CREATED ON
PURPOSE

—*for*—

PURPOSE

BECOMING GOD'S MASTERPIECE

LISA SINGH

Created on Purpose for Purpose

Copyright © 2015 Inspirations by Lisa

DEDICATION

I would like to dedicate this book to my wonderful husband and best friend, Nohar; my two beautiful children, Nicholas and Norah; and my HGM family for always being so supportive and encouraging, thus propelling me this far. My prayer is that the grace and peace of God be multiplied to you all. Love you guys always and forever!

TABLE OF CONTENTS

INTRODUCTION

I decided to put pen to paper because my heart was broken. I have been a Christian for twenty-three years and for eighteen of those years I lived a very defeated life. I had been in the "church world," so to speak, and found myself walking away feeling less able and capable of ever meeting God's demands. I attended meeting after meeting. I purchased any and every book, trying to find the answer to my broken heart and broken situation, yet always walking away with a temporary emotional fix.

One day I heard a message preached on the *Gospel of Grace*. I can't say that I fully embraced it, as the law (man's attempt to appease God by his efforts and works) was so embedded in me that I was very skeptical that it could be so easy to have a relationship with God apart from my works. But, somehow the Holy Spirit got a grip on my heart and spoke very gently to my spirit, "Give this a chance!" There was a struggle to take hold of it as the thoughts came to my mind that I should be careful of this *grace* teaching as it sounded like a trap to lead into sin. Despite the negative, God began to do a work on the inside of me that led me to a greater understanding of the finished work and person of Jesus Christ.

All the while, my pursuit of God was correct, but the motive of my heart was wrong. In spite of my overwhelming ignorance, God's grace was not exhausted. The Bible tells us "where sin abounds *grace* much more or super abounds" (Romans 5:20 AMP). In the midst of my journey of searching for Jesus, he found me. In being found by him, I received a new heart. I call it a "heart made for grace." Grace means undeserved or unearned favor; therefore, I received a heart made for underserved or unearned favor. It is no longer a question of "What do I need to do to be right with God" But it now becomes, "What has God done to make me right with himself?" Under the first question, I was not able to call God "father"; thereby, always having a feeling of distance, rejection, condemnation, and guilt. However, the second question brought me to a safe place of knowing that I was welcomed home—no distance, no rejection, no condemnation, and no guilt. The latter was, of course, greater in quantity and quality.

I started off saying my heart was broken; today it is still broken but not with the self-centered issues of feeling incapable to please God and a broken past. But now my heart breaks with the issues of God's children not being able to live in freedom because of the heavy burden of their past, and having no hope for the future. I wanted to write this book to help set God's children free—free from introspection, self-effort, defeat, worry, stress, anxiety, fear, condemnation, rejection, failure, and guilt. These very feelings are the enemy of the God-purpose for our lives, and I know our Father held back nothing good from us, but he put in motion his plan of reconciliation in order to establish a relationship with us, and the fact that we are not possessing this relationship with him, which in turn releases us into our inheritance, breaks his heart.

I pray that as you venture to read this book, that your life will be transformed by the power of the word and truth of God. I desire to present the simple yet very powerful good news made easy for you to grasp, take hold of, and be established in your life. At the end of every chapter there will be a list of, "Power Thoughts and Confessions." I did not just want to write a book for you to read, put it on the bookshelf, and move on, but I want this book to be a source of help to you. The Bible tells us that faith comes by hearing and hearing the spoken Word of God. Now, you will have the opportunity to build faith as *you believe and you speak* the Word over your life. I urge you not to rush through this book but take one chapter at a time and let it get into your heart because out of your heart flows life. Victory is already yours; Jesus paid a price for you to have it. My prayer is that you will also receive a heart made for grace that would propel you into manifesting your God-purpose!

CREATED ON PURPOSE
FOR PURPOSE

GOD DOES NOT CREATE ANYTHING INSIGNIFICANT, INFERIOR, OR WITHOUT A PURPOSE

God said, Let Us [Father, Son, and Holy Spirit] make mankind in Our image, after Our likeness, and let them have complete authority over the fish of the sea, the birds of the air, the [tame] beasts, and over all of the earth, and over everything that creeps upon the earth. So God created man in His own image, in the image and likeness of God He created him; male and female He created them. And God blessed them and said to them, Be fruitful, multiply, and fill the earth, and subdue it [using all its vast resources in the service of God and man]; and have dominion over the fish of the sea, the birds of the air, and over every living creature that moves upon the earth.

Genesis 1:26-28 (AMP)

For a very long time in my life I did not realize or understand the word *purpose*. In the Christian circle, purpose is a word that is used frequently, yet to me it was just a word. However, if we are to get where we are going in this life, purpose is the defining factor to the end result. On my new venture with my heavenly father, I began to get the clarity necessary for a successful journey and slowly realized the whole point of getting saved was not just to secure a spot in heaven when the Lord returns, but more so that I would be a living testimony for Jesus Christ. Let me explain—Jesus came to the earth to fulfill a specific purpose, which was to reconcile man to God. He spent the last three years of his life training his disciples to pick up the same cause and carry the good news to the ends of the earth, and as a result of his clear-cut God-purpose for which he came, it is still in effect even until today and will most definitely continue to be in effect until his return. Now, that is a God-purpose fulfilled! Sometimes it may take us a while to identify the God-purpose for our lives because of a lack of guidance or a godless upbringing, but that does not mean that the God-purpose does not exist. It would prove to be a cruel end if we were created just to pass time on the earth, experience hurts and pains, and then come to the end of the journey to find it all empty. I don't think this is the Creator of the universe's intentions because he is described as being love—it is who he is—and if this is his nature or very being, then creating something or someone for no purpose would be very hard to accept or comprehend.

Life is more than just passing through to get to a better place; even though that will be the end result, we have to believe that life is much more, and that the reason we were put on the earth is not to do time or to buy time but accomplish something with the time we have been given. We have to arrive at a place in our lives where we are convinced beyond the shadow of a doubt that we have been created on purpose for purpose! "On purpose" means intentional or deliberate. God's plan for creating us was intentional and deliberate, and there had to be a process of planning which would have crystallized the details for the finished product. I would like to encourage you to take a moment and think about the creation of your life, the science of it all, that out of millions of sperms racing for life, the one that contained you made it to the finish line. This thought alone is mind-boggling and should be imprinted in your thought pattern as you venture to launch into your God-purpose. My friends, I want to make this statement a personal one as you say it out loud so you can hear yourself, "I am created on purpose for purpose!"

From the outset, God states very clearly his purpose for mankind; there is no confusion or trial and error with God. He is all-knowing, all-powerful, and all-present, and that in itself tells us that he does not make mistakes. Sometimes people in our lives may say or do things that cause us to feel like we are mistakes, and this is a popular strategy used by the enemy to get us off our God-purpose and on a track to living a hopeless life. One of the things that I have noticed in my own life that hindered me from coming into my God-purpose was the teaching that led me to believe that unless I could attain a sinless life, I was not ever going to be success-ful in this life. This belief system was, and is, so flawed, that instead of me being empowered to fulfill the God-purpose, I was driven to despair because of my lack of ability to attain right standing with God. One of the most frustrating experi-ences in life was to have an idea that there was a purpose for your life, but not be equipped to achieve it. We must come to understand that where there is confusion about our direc-tion, there will be a delay in the moving forward process.

The children of Israel experienced wandering in the wil-derness for forty years because of a lack of confidence in their God. Unfortunately, they were never able to possess their promise and ultimately they missed fulfilling their God-purpose. If we are not willing to understand that God has a specific plan for our lives and he already equipped us to fulfill that plan, then we also will miss fulfilling our God-purpose in our lives. Thank God today our churches are raising up leaders that are infused with the wisdom of God to help lead his children into their destiny. And as the teach-ing that we were created on purpose for purpose comes to the forefront, there will definitely be less people wandering in the wilderness.

From the very beginning we can see the deliberate and intentional plan of God for our lives. God defines us and then he defines what we were created for. Unfortunately, we have been made to believe otherwise because the enemy knows that a believer who understands his God-purpose is a force to reckon with. That is why from our very inception the enemy launches his attacks on family units. Why? Because this is the most powerful unit that God created for his purpose to flow through. Usually a child that is subjected to a broken home, absentee parent, or abusive guardians tends to lose hope in their God-purpose, and is oftentimes caught in a constant state of chaos and confusion as to why they are here. The good news is that Jesus is coming back for a glorious church, and I believe we are living in an exciting time because the sleeping giant (the church) is now being quickened and becoming awake to bring the truth—which is the Word—to the forefront, thereby restoring the believer's God-purpose.

THE VESSEL TO ESTABLISH PURPOSE IS THE CHURCH

It is very difficult to give or receive love when you don't feel accepted, especially if you come from a broken home or abused relationship. God knows that we need to have patterns and examples in order to understand him and his love for us, hence the reason he lays out specific stories in his word on the father's love for the child and the husband's love for the wife. He established the family unit as an avenue for the father's love to flow to the child and the husband's love to flow to the wife.

Let us examine the father-son relationship in the life of Jesus. One day Jesus came to John the Baptist to be baptized at the Jordon River. After John had baptized Jesus, the heavens opened and John saw a dove descending upon Jesus, and then John heard God spoke, "This is My Son, My Beloved, in Whom I delight!" (Matthew 3:17 AMP). From this scripture we see an example of the father publicly declaring his love, acceptance, and approval of his son. It is also notable that Jesus officially began his ministry of preaching, teaching, and working of miracles after the spoken approval of his father. In the same way when a child hears that their parents are pleased and happy with them, it releases them into the realm of confidence and security; thereby propelling the child to be all that they were created to be. This declaration of approval from the parent to the child is one of the foundational elements in empowering a child to come into his or her God-purpose.

We also see the love of the father for the child in the story of the prodigal son told by Jesus (Luke 15:11-32). This story describes the unconditional love that a parent should possess for his or her child. In this story the prodigal son chooses a path that leads to rebellion and destruction, but it never stopped the father from loving his son. In fact, I believe it was this love that infused a hope in the father's heart and caused him to remain in faith, that his son would one day be restored. The story tells us when the son had practically hit rock bottom, eating pigs' food while taking care of pigs, he had an awakening in his soul. He then decided to go back home to his father, and the most beautiful description of unconditional love is portrayed. The story states, "So he got up and came to his [own] father. But while he was still a long way off, his father saw him and was moved with pity *and* tenderness [for him]; and he ran and embraced him and kissed him [fervently]" (Luke 15: 20 AMP). From this verse you can tell the father had to be looking out with expectation every day for his son. It was the father that saw his son in the distance and ran to him, but not only did he run to his son, he expressed his love for his son even though his son was not in the best condition physically, morally, or mentally. This story depicts the true essence of the love of a parent for a child. It is a love that never gives up but it drives the parent to keep praying and believing for the best in the child, no matter how far they may stray from the good path.

We also see the beautiful description of the husband relationship to the wife in the story of Ruth and Boaz (Ruth 2 AMP). Ruth was a young widowed woman who lived with her mother-in-law, Naomi, in Bethlehem. The times they lived in were much like the times we are facing now—there was a famine in the land. Boaz was wealthy but he was also compassionate; he provided for Ruth to glean from his field. He spoke kindly with Ruth even though she was a Moabite. He offered her protection from other men by allowing her to stay close to his maids. Boaz made sure that she knew she could drink water freely whenever she was thirsty. He was also very aware of the hardships she had faced with losing her husband but not neglecting her duty to her mother-in-law. He took time out to appreciate the sacrifices she made by not taking the option to go back to her parents but following Naomi to a land that was strange to her. And though she fell short of the required standards to marry Boaz, such as being a foreigner and widowed, he made a way to make sure he would marry her. The quality of the husband in this story is an example of what God wants existent in the marriage today. The husband should help provide physically for the home; he should provide protection and security for his wife and children; and he should show compassion, kindness, and appreciation for his wife. In today's society it sometimes takes both parents working to meet the needs of the household, but even with this being so, it still makes a big difference when the father and husband is present. And, again, I have to say the major unit that is affected in today's society is the family unit. With the family unit coming under attack constantly due to single parent homes or financial constraints, a breakdown of morals and family values transpires; thereby distorting the view and concept of God. When an earthly father or mother walks out of a child's life and does not look back, it causes the child to introspect and assign blame internally for that loss, and trusting becomes a task and a risk.

In my own life I can clearly recall how I felt when my father left me and never looked back. For a long time I blamed myself, by thinking I was not good enough for him to love, so he had to look for a way of escape. I did not know what it felt like to be hugged or to be carried in the arms of safety. There was a longing in my heart to hear the words, "I am proud of you" from my father, but to no avail. When my father did not return for many years, I was introduced to someone that would take his place, and that person was my stepfather. At the age of seven, I remember feeling desperate to have that father's embrace, and the feeling of protection that came with that embrace. Being that young my trust level in my stepfather was immense, but before long that trust came crashing down, due to the realization that he was an alcoholic. And to my dismay a new door was opened in my life for another phase of disappoints, hurts, shame, fear, and betrayal. All these feeling steamed from years of physical and mental abuse, and in my mind, I could not comprehend how a father-figure could misuse the trust of an innocent child.

But one day a Sunday school teacher came around to invite the kids in my neighborhood to come to church. And though I did not grasp the teachings at that time, this church became my safe haven. It was my home away from home. In order for healing and trust to be established again in the midst of all the brokenness, there has to be a place where stability and safety is constantly existent. And this place is known as the church.

In Dr. Marva Mitchell's book, *It Takes a Church To Raise a Village*, she states, "The village is no longer qualified or adequately prepared to raise a child because the village itself must be raised" (xxii). No longer will the church be defined as just a building that is beautified with stained glass windows and the highest steeple, or even the finest work of arts on the ceilings, or the padded pews. While all of this is nice, and we should take pride in the house in which we worship, it should not become the definition of the church. The church must be defined as the body of Christ. God has always been concerned about people and his heart is for his people to be taken care of by finding a safe haven within the walls of the church. It must now translate as a place of refuge and hope, a place of light and salvation, a place where hurting and broken people can feel the divine touch of God's hand through his children to bring change to lives. It is a place where people can feel like they were on a long journey and, finally, they are welcomed home. I experienced this feeling of being welcomed home in the church, because of one Sunday school teacher having a heart for the children in my community. In my desperate and broken state as a child, I could not reason for myself that I should go to church, but instead the church came to me. Fortunately for us, the church is becoming again the vessel by which God will raise the standard and put the examples back in the right order it was meant to be in.

This is taking place because the church has started moving outside of the four walls of the building and into the communities and homes of those in need. The outreach ministry of the church is a great way to get connected and offer hope to those in need by meeting the broken hearted at their doors and at their points of need through providing food, clothes, and everyday necessities. Only then will the avenues open up for us to bring the spiritual and soul healing by means of prayer, discipleship, and home cell groups, and eventually this will lead them to the local church. The church is equipped with the headship of Jesus Christ, so now the church must follow the pattern which Jesus Christ left for us. The Bible tells us that Jesus went about preaching, teaching, and healing all who were in need (Matthew 4:23 AMP). Jesus did go to the synagogue for service but when there was no service he went about being the church. When we the church start venturing out into the communities, and start meeting the needs of the broken hearts and homes, we will begin the process of healing the family unit. Then we will be able to raise strong believers that will be able to go into the world, which is in desperate need of a savior, and become the heart, hands, and face of Jesus Christ.

> And He has put all things under His feet and has appointed Him the universal and supreme Head of the church [a headship exercised throughout the church], Which is His body, the fullness of Him Who fills all in all [for in that body lives the full measure of Him Who makes everything complete, and Who fills everything everywhere with Himself]."

> Ephesians 1:22-23 (AMP)

Jesus Christ is the head of the church and the church must operate with this headship; he must be the centrality of everything the church does. The church cannot build up the name of men and place the titles of the offices higher than Jesus. The church cannot afford to barely mention Jesus's name here and there in a sermon, but all our sermons must be infused with the power of Jesus Christ and his resurrection. We are the bride and he is the bridegroom and when we allow human efforts and human wisdom to come under the headship of Jesus Christ; it's then, and only then, that broken lives be transformed and broken hearts be mended; thereby setting the stage for the imminent return for his bride (the church).

YOU WERE WELL THOUGHT-OUT

In being able to manifest our God-purpose we must first come to the realization that we are not a mistake or that we are not victims of chance or coincidence. But, in fact, we were a very thought in the mind of God. As God spoke to the young prophet Jeremiah, he said, "Before I shaped you in the womb, I knew all about you. Before you saw the light of day, I had holy plans for you: A prophet to the nations—that's what I had in mind for you" (Jeremiah 1:5 MSG).

God definitely thought us through and we are not a product of some big explosion that happened in space. We are created in the very image of God and we most definitely have a God-purpose to fulfill. The enemy loves and thrives on feeding us lies that keep our potentials dwarfed. His lies come in the form of words and statements that are spoken over our lives from people who hold a position of influence such as family members, guardians, teachers, and even peers. Many times these individuals have no clue that they are being used by the enemy, so holding or carrying a grudge against these people is yet another tactic of the enemy to keep us in bondage. Some of the lies the enemy uses are statements like, "You don't matter in this life," or "Nothing good could ever come from you, that is why your parents left you," or "You are insignificant because your family background is poor and uneducated and you are going to follow that same path." He uses statements like, "You are ugly or fat or stupid or slow." Even though these may seem like simple words, when they are spoken by someone in authority over your life they become very weighty words that shape your outlook and overview of life.

Our words are so very powerful and we will look at the power of the spoken word in a later chapter, but for now we must engrave in our minds the words that God has spoken over us. When you gain a personal revelation that the Creator, made heaven and earth and also took time to think about you as an individual, you will not be able to deny your purpose, and with that revelation comes resolve to accomplish that purpose for which you were created. He thought about the gifting and talents he would deposit in us before the foundation of the earth. There is no other you and no one else can do what he created you to do. With man, you may be dispensable, but with God you will always be indispensable.

Do not give up on your dreams that may have died along the way, but hold on to hope that the purpose for which you were created will become a reality. Just because you have not seen the reality of the God-purpose for your life does not mean that it is not there; this is where the opportunity for your faith in God's abilities to manifest has to come to the forefront. The plan of God for your life is very clear, and as we look at the life of Jesus we will be able to see the plan and purpose more and more until it forms the whole picture. The Apostle Paul describes it this way:

> God knew what he was doing from the very beginning. He decided from the outset to shape the lives of those who love him along the same lines as the life of his Son. The Son stands first in the line of humanity he restored. We see the original and intended shape of our lives there in him. After God made that decision of what his children should be like, he followed it up by calling people by name. After he called them by name, he set them on a solid basis with himself. And then, after getting them established, he

stayed with them to the end, gloriously complet-
ing what he had begun.

Romans 8:29-30 (MSG)

HE GIVES US HELP

After the fall of man in the Garden of Eden, the world in
which we live in also became a part of the fallen state. This
condition of the system did not alter God's original plan for
our lives, but instead he made a way for this plan to manifest, and that was through his Son, Jesus Christ. God's kingdom is opposed to the kingdoms of this world, and because
we live in this fallen world we still have to deal with natural
circumstances that are opposed to the will and purposes of
God. Knowing your position in Christ will always give you
the advantage over the enemy because many of us know that
the main weapon of the enemy is launched against the mind
of the believer. Our heavenly father was not caught off-guard
by this attack, but he also knew that by ourselves we would
never be able to win this fight, hence the reason he gave us a
helper—the Holy Spirit.

> But the Comforter (Counselor, Helper, Interces-
> sor, Advocate, Strengthener, Standby), the Holy
> Spirit, Whom the Father will send in My name
> [in My place, to represent Me and act on My be-

half], He will teach you all things. And He will cause you to recall (will remind you of, bring to your remembrance) everything I have told you.

John 14:26 (AMP)

God knows we cannot function in this world without his help and as a result he does not leave us stranded or alone. He wants us to succeed, prosper, and rise above every situation that would pose potential threats in fulfilling our God-purpose. God did not just send anyone, he sent the Holy Spirit, which is the very spirit of Christ himself. Knowing this truth is half the battle won on our behalf, because many times we are trying to go about this life in our strength and our knowledge, and the truth is that we don't have what it takes to survive. The Holy Spirit is not just our helper, he is our defender—he fights for us and on our behalf. He is also given to us to teach us about everything pertaining to Jesus and his Word, as well as everyday life issues. Many of us think that we are alone, and when challenges arise we become fearful and we see failure because we don't realize that we have help. The helper who is the Holy Spirit is also the third person of the God-head, and he knows the will of God for our lives, and if he knows the perfect will of God for us, then it would do us good to embrace fully all the help we have been given.

The Holy Spirit teaches us, comforts us, and he helps us to pray the will of God for our lives; he is always with us and he is given to stay with us forever. My friends, you are never ever alone once you are in Christ Jesus. With the help of the Holy Spirit we can counteract the attacks of the enemy through his leading and teachings of the truth of God's Word. When this happens, faith is established in the believer's life, and taking God's promises to heart is not secondary, but the primary source of our manifesting purpose. God himself spoke this promise to Jeremiah, "I know what I'm doing. I have it all planned out—plans to take care of you, not abandon you, plans to give you the future you hope for" (Jeremiah 29:11, MSG).

God knows what he is doing when it concerns his children, and he has no intentions of leaving us alone to fight our way through, but, rather, he is going to be there every step of the way, leading and guiding us to the end. It is about time the believer learned this very powerful truth that the very spirit of Christ is with us and he doesn't come and go but is always there. When we start to pay attention to him and enlist his help in every situation, then and only then will we become equipped to overcome this fallen system. When we become aware that the Holy Spirit is given to help us and guide us, a lot of confusion in our lives will be eliminated. Sometimes we may feel fearful about change, like a promotion on the job, and if we pray and ask the Holy Spirit to help us, he will use the simplest of methods to assure us all will be well. He knows our struggles, and sometimes he would use friends to send us a text or an e-mail on a story or scripture that somehow helps to alleviate the fear we were feeling. The Holy Spirit will always remind us of the righteousness we have in Christ, and he does so by the word of God, be it through a daily devotional, the Bible, a social network status, or just a friend. Whatever your struggle, be it worry, fear, anxiety, or condemnation, just ask the Holy Spirit to help you. Once he knows we are depending on him he will show us the way to the truth always.

POWER THOUGHTS AND CONFESSIONS

I am created on purpose for purpose.

I am not insignificant, inferior, or without a purpose.

I don't just have a purpose, but I have a God-purpose.

I am part of the vessel, which establishes purpose, and that is the church.

I was well thought-out by God.

God's plans for me are all good.

I have help from God to accomplish my God-purpose and he is the Holy Spirit.

WHAT IS OUR GOD-PURPOSE?

But you shall receive power (ability, efficiency, and might) when the Holy Spirit has come upon you, and you shall be My witnesses in Jerusalem and all Judea and Samaria and to the ends (the very bounds) of the earth.

Acts 1:8 (AMP)

TO BE WITNESSES

We all have been equipped with certain gifts and talents by God to accomplish our purpose, and it all leads to one specific end, and that is to be a witness for him. Every one of us was created to be a witness for Jesus. The world is multifaceted and multicultural; we are not all the same—that is why we all have different strong points embedded in us. It does not mean that once we become a Christian that we have to leave our jobs and families and go off on some mission to a country to help the poor. While helping poor people should be our concern and considering the experience of a mission trip in the future could prove to be beneficial to our world view of poverty. God does not expect us to leave life as we know it unless there is a specific call on our lives for missions. God knows we have responsibilities to our family, church, and community as a whole. But his purpose is for us to use the platform we have been given through our talents and gifting to be a witness right where we are. So it does not matter what field we may be in, the fact is, this specific field now transforms into a witnessing field. For example, if you are a business owner, your business now becomes a platform for you to be a witness for Christ. You will have both employees and customers to relate to, and though your main goal is to be successful in your business, at the same time you want to fulfill your God-purpose. With this mindset of being a witness you can now use every opportunity to exude Christ. In just the simple way of giving instructions to your employees, instead of being harsh in your tone, you can use a soft tone with kind words. Your kind words can change the whole day of someone who might have left home that morning having an argument with their spouse or child and were upset internally. Your kind words can offer hope to someone who is mistreated by others on the job or outside the job. Your kind words can add value to a person's life as stated in the book of Proverbs; "A soft answer turns away wrath, but grievous words stir up anger" (Proverbs 15:1 AMP).

Oftentimes you will have to make decisions pertaining to the direction of the business; taking time to listen to the issues that may bother both your staff and customers will cause you to make better decisions. Also, in taking the time to listen, you will add value to the people that are around you, and when they feel valued by you, they will perform better on their jobs as well.

Another way you can use your business as a platform to be a witness is by extending monetary help to ministries that do missions to other nations. Though you cannot go yourself, you will be helping to provide for the missionaries that are called to this area. When you give to missions financially, people from the outside may not see it. But we have an assurance that when we give for the Lord's work, it will be given back unto us in abundance (Luke 6:38 AMP). Because of this promise, people will be able to see your business prospering and being successful. Now, if they should ask, "What is your secret to success?" a door is now opened for you to share your testimonies of God's goodness to you and your business. It really does not matter what area of life we might be operating in, we can take the opportunity to turn our platform into a mission field for Christ.

The idea is that while we are operating in our purpose in life we are fulfilling the God-purpose, by using our natural talents, such as leadership skills, artistic skills, compassion, kindness, and even encouragement to glorify God and lead others to him.

God makes our part so easy once we get to know him. God has many beautiful treasures hidden in his Word, but it is not hidden from us, it is hidden for us so that we may make a conscious effort to seek it out. Our witnessing will be seen by the world not because of what we say or how much we say, but, truly, the world will see actual evidence in our lives that they will not be able to dispute our God being real and being with us. We were created to be witnesses to the truth that God is a real father and he cares about his children, but more than caring is the truth that he loves us, and this love is beyond earning or repayment. Out of his love for us he gave us the gift of new life and this new life opens a door to new opportunities for others to experience his love in the same measure.

As believers we need to have a revelation that this time on earth is only as it suggests—for a time, and then there is life after, but while here, God wants us to be good stewards of time. Our purpose is not to spend all our time trying to make millions that we won't have time to enjoy other areas of life. He wants us to have a balanced life and that includes a family, a job, good health, and wealth, but in the middle of it all he must take center position, and when it is ordered this way, all our needs and wants will flow in automatically. We cannot be good witnesses if we are sick or financially stressed or in a bad mood. In order to represent the goodness and favor of God, his very personality must shine through us, and only then will we be able to effect changes in others around us. Jesus describes it this way: You are the light of the world. A city set on a hill cannot be hidden. Nor do men light a lamp and put it under a peck measure, but on a lampstand, and it gives light to all in the house. Let your light so shine before men that they may see your moral excellence and your praiseworthy, noble, and good deeds and recognize and honor and praise and glorify your Father Who is in heaven.

Matthew 5:14-16 (AMP)

Our sole and ultimate purpose is to be a witness to the world around us by revealing to them that our father is God, and that he is real and active in our lives. When we come into the full revelation that we were created to be a witness that would lead others to the truth about God, then we would also be successful in leading them into a relationship with God. God has always been interested in a relationship with his children, and when we come into our God-purpose we eventually help others to do the same. The world does not pay attention to what we say, but they will stop and take notice by what they see. Therefore, we must produce fruit in our lives. The witnessing life must be a fruit-bearing life.

When a tree bears fruit, we notice, because the tree is covered in it. Imagine with me for a moment that we are going apple picking and as we enter the field there is a wide expanse of trees just laden with apples. It almost seems impossible that we could ever pick all of that fruit, and the colors radiating from the trees are so breathtaking. Well, the life of the believer should reflect the very image of the tree that is ready for the picking, loaded with the fruit of love, joy, peace, patience, kindness, goodness, faithfulness, gentleness, and self-control (Galatians 5:22 AMP). In studying the Word for myself I have come to realize that there are three areas the world looks at in the believer's life that will eventually cause them to make a decision for or against a relationship with Jesus Christ. The world looks at the believer to see how we operate in our God-purpose as we, dominate over creation, relate to people, and exercise control over ourselves.

1) GOD CREATED US TO HAVE DOMINION OVER THE EARTH

> And God blessed them and said to them, Be fruitful, multiply, and fill the earth, and subdue it [using all its vast resources in the service of God and man]; and have dominion over the fish of the sea, the birds of the air, and over every living creature that moves upon the earth.
>
> Genesis 1:28 (AMP)

The world is looking at us to see how we deal with dominion. Many times we try to stay away from the word *dominion* because it carries a negative connotation. Isn't it just like the enemy to distort the things of God? But God created us to have dominion over the earth and its resources and also to be in charge of all the animals.

The problem came in after the fall of man and now instead of us dominating over creation, man desired to dominate over other people. It was never meant to be this way as all people are created equal in the sight of God, and we all need his help to continue to be sustained. But instead of our focus being on God, man became prideful and greedy and power hungry, thereby causing him to want to control people through the means of manipulation for selfish gains. As a result of this domination, men no longer had equal rights, but discrimination and injustice ruled. Jesus came and completed the work of redemption, and equality was re-established at the foot of the cross. This act put the children of God back in a position to view all men as having value and worth. When we proclaim to the world that we are followers of Christ, we are, in fact, proclaiming that we see value in all men and we are motivated by love toward them. When we treat all men with value, we are in actuality declaring that we view them as God would view them. When the world sees believers treating other people with value and worth, and going out of their way to lend a helping hand to those in need, then they will stop and take notice of the God we serve.

As I have mentioned before, it is not how much we say or what we say, it is what the world sees in us that will make the difference. When we stop trying to control people and instead have compassion for them, then we will start functioning in our God-purpose. When we can start using our resources for the service of God and men, then we will be on the path of fulfilling our God-purpose.

2) GOD CREATED US TO REIGN IN THIS LIFE AS KINGS THROUGH JESUS CHRIST

> For if because of one man's trespass (lapse, offense) death reigned through that one, much more surely will those who receive [God's] overflowing grace (unmerited favor) and the free gift of righteousness [putting them into right standing with Himself] reign as kings in life through the one Man Jesus Christ (the Messiah, the Anointed One).
>
> Romans 5:17 (AMP)

The next aspect that the world will stop and pay attention to in the believer's life is the fact that we are reigning as kings in life. For a king to reign in life he must first come from a royal line, having more than enough, and possessing authority and wisdom to make decisions that would lead others into victory. He has to be confident in the kingdom he represents, carrying and bearing his father's name with honor and value; he must uphold a flawless character, being one that many will aspire to be like; he is the ultimate role model for every young man and a prize for every young lady. He possesses charm and charisma that draws the attention of a whole room with his presence; and he is able to silence his critics with the victories that are produced from his leadership. His words are very weighty and determine the outcome of the future for his kingdom and the lives he represents and defends. In today's world this description seems difficult to live up to especially if you did not come from a royal family. Unfortunately, the standards by which the world judges importance and value tend to come from a prestigious family name, monetary wealth, status, and position in society. And as a result of this measurement of importance by the world standards, many believers end up living defeated, unhappy lives.

For a very long time I lived like this because I came from a poor family, and as a result, education was not a priority. I was always behind on my school work, and I found myself in a place of always comparing myself to those who seemed to have it all together. I used the sorry circumstances of poverty and lack to dominate my way of thinking. As a result of this thinking, the view of me was one of very low self-esteem, and this view caused me to be overwhelmingly depressed. With the absence of a family name and wealth, I ventured out to establish my own legacy. My view was if I could work hard enough, acquire more skills, and increase in education I would finally have a position in society that I earned. I learned to swim, I learned first aid, I learned to cook special dishes and bake a variety of desserts, I learned cosmetology, I studied to become a kindergarten teacher, I studied for fashion designing, I studied for the travel business, and finally I went to Bible college. At the end of all of this I still was not reigning in life because anger, hurts, bitterness and un-forgiveness dominated me. It seemed like I had hit a dead end every single time. And the more certificates I added the more bad attitudes I added as well. I became proud because of my achievements, and I prized myself above others because of my abilities. Don't get me wrong, having goals in life is necessary for our growth, but our worth and value should not come from our achievements. Our achievement does add to our abilities, but it will not give us inner peace and cause us to reign over soul issues in life. All the while I was on this road to achievement I still displayed anger, rebellion, and selfishness, and the people around me could clearly see it.

The *grace* teaching truly opened my eyes to where my worth was really found and that was in the blood line of Jesus. I started to gain revelation that I did come from royalty as the Apostle Peter stated,

> But you are a chosen race, a royal priesthood, a dedicated nation, [God's] own purchased, special people, that you may set forth the wonderful deeds *and* display the virtues and perfections of Him Who called you out of darkness into His marvelous light.
>
> 1 Peter 2:9 (AMP)

I started searching out the scriptures that revealed to me who I was, not by my achievements but who I was in conjunction to Jesus Christ. The book of Ephesians truly did an unveiling for me, and I started to see myself as God sees me, being seated with Christ in the heavenly realms far above every principality, power, and name that we deem as powerful on this earth (Ephesians 1 AMP).

As I began to understand this position I have in Christ I was now able to grasp the underlying issues in my life, such as the hurts, pains, disappointment, and bitterness and bring them in prayer to the Lord. I started praying the promises of God, like, "I know the plans I have for you and they are good plans" (Jeremiah 29:11), and "You shall be the head and not the tail, above only and not beneath" (Deuteronomy 28:13 AMP). And supernaturally it seemed, as I prayed the words of God over my life, the issues that plagued me for years started disappearing, and the rebellious heart I had started to become soft with kindness and compassion. For the first time in my life I was able to experience freedom from the past and self-achievement, and only when you are free you will be empowered to reign in life. Reigning in this life is not limited to having material possessions in abundance but being able to reign over life issues that once kept us blind to our savior.

This is the very description and prototype of the believer that knows their God and is operating in their God-purpose. We should possess the revelation of who we are in Christ and understand the royal line that we are now representing. The world will not want to take this walk with us if we do not possess the attributes of our father. They want to see that we are confident in the authority we have been given, yet compassionate enough to stop and speak a kind word or offer a smile along the way. We have to come to a point where we are reigning over material possessions instead of being ruled by them. We are blessed with all the blessings of God and we crystallize God's reputation when we walk in his blessings. We should be able to reign over sickness and disease, poverty and stress, anger, bitterness, and negativity; always being a source of help to others, building them up instead of bringing them down, being kind to someone even when we know they are undeserving. When we decide to walk in our God-purpose, we will be able to open up God's vault and become rich in hope, faith, and love, having a positive outlook on life no matter how bad the situations may become. Why? Because we understand our position in this life depends solely on our position in Christ.

3) GOD CREATED US TO PROSPER IN OUR SOUL

"Beloved, I pray that you may prosper in every way and [that your body] may keep well, even as [I know] your soul keeps well and prospers."

3 John 1:2 (AMP)

The third aspect that the world stops to take notice of in the believer's life is how we are as individuals. Everyone can tell if a person is prosperous materially because there will be evidence presented by the grandeur of their house, the job and position they hold in their occupational field, or by the car they drive and the clothes they wear. The world has no problem identifying this kind of prosperity, but this is not a balanced prosperity. The Apostle John's prayer for us as believers is that we prosper in our souls as well as our bodies, and from this we can understand that prosperity goes beyond material possessions.

A prosperous soul is so important to manifesting our God-purpose that I have dedicated a whole chapter to address this. The world looks also at the way we exercise self-control or how we handle stress on the job or patience with our children. They look at us to see if we have anger issues or if we are obscene in our speech. Whether we like it or not, the world is ready to judge the believer very harshly because they know better than us the fruit that should be present in a godly person, even though they themselves are not following God. The stakes and expectation of the believer is set very high by the world and they will take every opportunity to cut us down. Our focus should not be on our works, but our focus should be on living a life that glorifies God, and when our focus remains this way we inevitably produce lives that emanate the God-life.

The soul is the major focus of this book because it is the area that needs to become healthy. So often we spend a whole lot of time fixing the body through exercise, cosmetics, grooming, and healthy eating, but our hearts do not experience the peace that Jesus died to give us. When the world sees a believer that can have a smile and keep a positive vocabulary amidst an economic depression, they will take notice. When the world sees the believer being able to remain happy and joyful even though his boss is in a bad mood, or they see us being hopeful for God's best, even when we don't see it, or when they see us trusting God to supply our needs even when we receive a pay cut, then we will be on the road to accomplishing our God-purpose. God wants the best for us and his best for us does not start from the outside in but rather from the inside out. Let us embrace this new journey of walking out our God-purpose by becoming the best witness we can be with all the help given to us by God. Let us as individuals join together, learn how to become prosperous in our souls, and set this world on fire for Jesus. Let us be the lamps that are glowing from the mountaintops—that bring light and hope to this dying world.

POWER THOUGHTS AND CONFESSIONS

My ultimate God-purpose is to be a witness for God.

I was created to have dominion over the resources and created things of the earth.

I will use the resources given to me in the service of God and his people.

I was not created to pass time or do time on the earth.

I will use time to accomplish my God-purpose today.

I proclaim that I will be the best witness for God that I can be.

I will use the platform of my natural talent to glorify God and lead others to him.

I will reign in this life as a king because I am in Christ Jesus.

I will prosper in my soul, mind, will, and emotions.

I will be part of the body of Christ that sets this world on fire for Jesus.

RECONSTRUCTION

Reconstruction is a very necessary part of fulfilling the God-purpose in our lives. At the point of getting saved or being born again, Jesus comes into our lives and takes up residence in our spirit man. God created us tripartite—spirit, soul, and body. The original intent was for the spirit of man to always dominate and dictate the flow of man's daily life because man communicated with God through his spirit. There is a void in man's spirit waiting to be filled and that void can only be filled with God—hence the reason man is constantly trying to satisfy this void by adopting and experimenting with all sorts of different drugs, philosophies, multiple partners, and even religion that lead only to a dead end.

You see, man is a spirit who has a soul, which lives in a body. The body that everyone sees is the house for the real person. So at the fall in the garden of Eden, man's spirit died. That is why there are so many different religions, practices, spiritualism, ideologies, and fantasies, because the human spirit is desperate for the void to be filled. And unless the gospel of Jesus Christ comes to the forefront, people will continue to embrace any and every whim and fancy to find satisfaction. Once Jesus is preached and accepted, His spirit (the Holy Spirit) moves into our spirit, bringing us to life again, and it is in this condition that man can commune with and worship God. Because God is a spirit, our worship cannot be effective via any other means; we now have to be able to communicate with God through our spirit that is infused and alive with Christ. The Apostle John said it this way, "God is a Spirit (a spiritual Being) and those who worship Him must worship Him in spirit and in truth (reality)" (John 4:24 AMP).

Truly there was a lot of damage done to the human race from that one simple act by Adam and Eve. This one act of disobedience put the entire human race on a path of decay. This decaying pattern gives the idea of total ruin unless something is put in place not only to stop the decay but to cause an actual reversal of this process. And this, my friends, is the good news that gives us hope and strength to carry on even in the midst of a decaying world. God instituted a plan that would undo what the first Adam did by sending the second Adam to take our place. Our second Adam is Jesus, according to Romans 5:15 (AMP). Now, because of the finished work of Jesus Christ at the cross, we have been equipped with the abilities to reconstruct our brokenness and decaying mental process to one of wholeness, health, freedom, and newness of life.

OLD THINGS ARE PASSED AWAY

The old order and way of thinking must change, but, unfortunately, the manifestation of the newness of life does not happen overnight. Can it? Sure it can, with God all things are possible, but God is interested in relationships. He is interested in a relationship that is built on a solid foundation of us trusting him in every small detail of our lives—hence, the reason our journey with God is a progressive one that is built precept upon precept. I used to be very disillusioned in my life because I expected every problem I had in life to disappear because I was now in a relationship with the God of the universe. However, today, after much pain and heartache from my own misconception of God, I have come to understand that the problems of this life will still be around, but with God on the inside of me and knowing that Jesus overcame this world, I have courage and strength that I too can come through any problem. As a matter of fact, I see every problem now as an opportunity for God to show forth his power in my life. But in order to come to this stage we have to do some reconstructing to our present state in order to experience the fullness of the God-purpose in our lives.

When we think about reconstructing something, we get the picture of an already present structure—let's take for example a house that has been around but has been abandoned. Does the house exist? Yes, and we see the structure from the outside. It may look like a house, but because of neglect or the lack of permanent occupants, there may be cracks or holes that developed because of the changes of the weather or seasons. And on the inside the condition may appear worse due to being left unattended for a long period of time—it may be dirty, there might be rats and rodents that carry diseases, and there might be water leaks that leave stains on the floors, walls, and ceilings. The good news is that someone came along, saw the house, thought to themselves that there is potential for this house, that it could become livable again, it could be cleaned out and fumigated, and they decided to pay a price for a broken down, ugly, filthy, decaying house. The person did not see the present state but chose to look at what could be if they moved in as opposed to the natural state at the present.

But what if the person bought the house, moved in, did not do any reconstruction to the house, and just lived in it in the same condition they bought it in? Well, the decaying process would continue, the house would become dirtier, and they would probably become infected by diseases; even though they have the resources available to make the changes by cleaning up the house, they refuse to use the resources and so they live a very unhealthy and degenerated lifestyle.

My friends, our bodies are the house; our soul is the inside of the house; and our spirit is where the Holy Spirit takes up residence. Jesus came along and saw what we could be like if he was to move into our lives. He saw the potential of us becoming clean and healthy once he moved into our spirits, and with him taking up residence in our spirits he also brought with him every single tool and resource necessary for us to clean up the rest of our house (soul). Now, we have to take the recourses and use them in the reconstructing process, and we start with the inside because we all know that what is reflected on the outside is a result of what is really happening on the inside. God gave the children of Israel a choice of life or death and asked them to choose. He has also given us a choice and we have to make a decision as believers to embrace the reconstructing process which begins in the soul—the inside of the house.

A PROSPEROUS SOUL
(MIND, WILL, AND EMOTIONS)

After you have invited Jesus to come into your heart, to take center place in your life, the question remains, "Now what?" The truth is that you have become born again, which means your spirit man has become alive, and this enables you to communicate with God freely through Jesus Christ, as well as secures your place with him after this life on earth. But, the fact remains that you still have to live in this fallen world, and the nature of this fallen world is in direct opposition to God's way. You still have to deal with the soul, which consists of the mind, will, and emotions. In today's world a lot of emphasis is placed on the body or outward man—looks, physique, healthy eating, anti-aging products, new fitness programs, fashion, cosmetic surgery and the list goes on and on. It is a clear indication that we are over compensating the external needs while neglecting the inner man-the soul, where the real issues exist. Again I will go back to the example of the house. What good is it if we move into the house and then venture to only put a pretty coat of paint on the outside and neglect the inside with all the filthy garbage, leaky stains, and disease-carrying rodents? It makes no sense to polish the outside when there are real issues going on inside the house where we have to spend most of our time.

In reality, the true source of many of our problems as believers is the fact that we are putting on pretty coats of paint on the outside, trying to convince everyone else that we have it all together because we don't want to be branded as not being able to keep up with society. We keep hiding the problems on the inside because it seems as if no one will ever be able to know we are real people with real issues, because that would only present us as being weak. This pressure of keeping up appearances on the outside really forces us to live a life that is very superficial, and the end result is emptiness. When we are alone we enter in the house and all the unresolved issues are patiently awaiting us; this is why God wants us to get his order correct. He wants us to change from the inside out; he wants the house that he lives in and you live in to come into the fullest potential that he knows is there. The one thing that we should realize is that Jesus does not send us on our own, he moves in with us to help us along the way as we do the reconstruction necessary to accomplish our God-purpose. The truth is, once you have a prosperous soul, it will trickle down to a prosperous body, thereby eliminating the need for all the excessive material stuff. It is God's will for us to prosper not only outwardly, but first inwardly. The Apostle John states it like this, "Beloved, I pray that you may prosper in all things and be in health, just as your *soul* prospers" (3 John 1:2, NKJV).

THE NEW COVENANT BELIEVER'S WORK IS TO "BELIEVE AND SPEAK!"

Everything about God is life and life giving, and I love that about him. In the beginning God created the heavens and the earth and he put man in the midst of an already prepared garden. Life was beautiful, but then came the fall. All of a sudden there was death all around. Instead of looking at life issues God's way, we now see life issues the enemy's way and that is why reconstruction is necessary. Fortunately for us, as I mentioned earlier, we have the very help of Jesus (the Holy Spirit). For a long time I would read the Word of God and I was taught that I have to confess the Word, it would change the situations in my life. I know many of you reading this book were taught the same thing. But for many years I would confess the Word over dead situations in my life and nothing changed. Of course this system was based on a shaky foundation because after a while of speaking and not seeing the results, I would become very frustrated and give up, and even blame God sometimes for his lack of concern for me. No doubt the enemy was having a field day at my expense because he loves a believer who has no revelation of the truth. And the truth is that salvation starts with hearing the good news, believing the good news, and then confessing the good news. We are saved by grace through faith.

> For with the heart a person believes (adheres to, trusts in, and relies on Christ) and so is justified (declared righteous, acceptable to God), and with the mouth he confesses (declares openly

and speaks out freely his faith) and confirms [his] salvation.

Romans 10:10 (AMP)

From the verse above we now see very clearly the pattern for how the believer should live his newfound life in God, and it is very simple—first we believe and then we speak. After much failure in my own life of speaking but not seeing any results, I went to the Lord with the question *why?* And while studying the topic of the thought life, I remember his response was crystal clear—I don't think I had ever heard the Lord so clearly in my life before—and this is what he said to me, "Your speaking is ineffective because your thinking is corrupted."

I was shocked at his response, but it did change my life. You see, confessing the Word without the right believing pattern is no different from trying to stay alive without breathing. Our thinking must line up with our speaking. We cannot have a picture of failure and be speaking success; a picture of sickness and speaking health; or a picture of death and speaking life. We must have the life thought pattern, and then we will be able to speak life and see life. So, all the while I was speaking the blessings I wanted to see but my thought pattern and mental pictures were the very opposite of those blessings. For example, I would be speaking the blessing that, "My God shall supply all my needs according to his riches in glory" (Philippians 4:19 AMP), but then I would listen to the news reports that would show the unemployment rate rising, and suddenly my thoughts would wander off into thinking, what if my husband has to close the business? How would we pay for tuition for the kids? Or how would we continue to maintain health insurance. As a result of this thought pattern, I would find myself in feelings of fear and anxiety about the future, which caused my words to be ineffective.

Our God is a God of order and when he set order in place, nothing and no one can alter it. And though this principle of believing and speaking might seem so simple, it will do us good not to underestimate the abundant power that flows from it. Our thought life is so powerful that it could decide our present disposition in life and also determine the direction of our future. Pondering the power of our thought life should cause us to want to reconstruct our souls. We all have a soul, but it is not enough to have a soul; as believers we should desire a prosperous soul, after all, the Bible tells us that we are what we think upon, "For as he thinks in his heart, so is he" (Proverbs 23:7, AMP).

There is only one thing that can truly reconstruct the thought life and that is the Word of God. Because we are living in a fallen world, it requires power from the inside out to combat the negatives that originate from this fallen state, and the only thing powerful enough to combat the negatives is the inspired and God-breathed Word.

POWER THOUGHTS
AND CONFESSIONS

I am made in the image of God and I consist of spirit, soul, and body.

I will worship God in spirit and in truth.

I am in the process of reconstruction.

Old thoughts and ways are passed away and I will operate under the new things of God.

I declare that my soul—mind, will, and emotions are prosperous.

My work as a new covenant believer is to *believe and speak* the Word of God.

I am what I think and today I choose to think on the promises of God.

RECONSTRUCTING THE MIND

HOW DO WE CHANGE OUR THOUGHT PATTERNS?

Do not be conformed to this world (this age), [fashioned after and adapted to its external, superficial customs], but be transformed (changed) by the [entire] renewal of your mind [by its new ideals and its new attitude], so that you may prove [for yourselves] what is the good and acceptable and perfect will of God, even the thing which is good and acceptable and perfect [in His sight for you].

Romans 12:2 (AMP)

When we speak about changing our minds, it carries with it the connotation of something existing permanently, but the content changes. For example, your skull contains your brain and your brain contains your thoughts. You cannot go to the store and buy a new skull with a new brain; you take the permanent skull and brain and you change the thought patterns that are there. This term is also called repentance. The word translated *repent* in the English New Testament is the Greek word *metanoeo*.

Vine's Concise Dictionary says *metanoeo,* means to perceive afterwards; hence, it signifies to change one's mind or purpose, and it always involves a change for the better.

From this definition of repentance, we can now fully understand Romans 12:2—renewing the mind for the better life God originally had for us. Now that we have established this basic fact of repentance, we can move on to the actual renewing process. Many times believers walk away disappointed and frustrated because they want things done instantly. It is almost as if we live in the microwave age, and everything must happen quickly and instantly or else it is not God. On the contrary, God is here to stay in our lives, and renewing our minds involves building, setting foundation, and then building layer upon layer that causes what we build to remain. I want to encourage you to stick with the Lord because He never disappoints. He is faithful, and if he said it he will do it.

> BLESSED (happy, fortunate, prosperous, and enviable) is the man who walks and lives not in the counsel of the unGodly [following their advice, their plans and purposes], nor stands [submissive and inactive] in the path where sinners walk, nor sits down [to relax and rest] where the scornful [and the mockers] gather. But his delight and desire are in the law of the Lord, and on His law (the precepts, the instructions, the teachings of God) he habitually meditates (ponders and studies) by day and by night.

And he shall be like a tree firmly planted [and tended] by the streams of water, ready to bring forth its fruit in its season; its leaf also shall not fade or wither; and everything he does shall prosper [and come to maturity].

Psalm 1: 1-3 (AMP)

Let us take a closer look at the scripture above as we explore the simple keys to renewing the mind.

KEY #1—YOU WILL HAVE TO DISCONNECT FROM DOING THINGS THE OLD WAY—ACCORDING TO THE WORLD SYSTEM

BLESSED (happy, fortunate, prosperous, and enviable) is the man who walks and lives not in the counsel of the ungodly [following their advice, their plans and purposes], nor stands [submissive and inactive] in the path where sinners walk, nor sits down [to relax and rest] where the scornful [and the mockers] gather.

Psalm 1:1(AMP)

If we are going to have a prosperous mind we have to change our habits. We cannot continue the same routines as before. If we do, then we will be doomed to fail. Do I have to be cut off from the world and go up to a mountain and live a life for God in quiet and stillness in order to renew my mind? No, that may not be possible for many of us as we still have to work and take care of our families and exist in this world, but we now have to take certain precautions that we did not take before. If you used to hang out at the bar with your friends and have a few beers and ended up cheating on your wife, this would be something you would have to cut out of your life. If you have a problem with credit card debt, especially going shopping when bad things happen to you as a comfort, then avoiding the shopping areas for a while would be a wise choice. If you have a problem with pornography, then locking down the computer for a while would be a good idea. If you have a problem with consulting with the astrologer or horoscopes for insight into the future, then this would be something you want to stay away from.

So, by the few things I just listed, you get the idea of some of the simple precautions you would have to take in order to get on the road to a healthy, renewed mind. I know saying these solutions are usually easier than doing them, especially when these habits seem to be so rooted in us, but the good news is that Jesus has already conquered these habits for us and he put us on the winning side. Making a few small adjustments would only benefit us in the long run. Many times we don't like change because we view change as something that obstructs our comfort level. No one likes to be uncomfortable, but if we look at our lives as a whole and not just in fragments then we get the bigger picture, and this bigger picture includes the end result of

God's plan and purpose for our lives. It is the bigger picture that enables us to embrace the changes that need to be implemented because we are now working toward fulfilling the God-purpose for our lives.

CHOICES DETERMINE THE CONSEQUENCES

One of the most powerful attributes of the individual is the power to choose. God designed us with a free choice because there is nothing more awesome than knowing someone loves or worships God, not because they are being forced to, but from the millions of paths to go, we choose to go God's way. We are faced with choices all the time, and these choices determine the consequences. The good news is that what the Lord asks us to do is simple and doable, and it benefits us in the long run. At some point in our lives, if we want to see the victory manifested that Christ already died to give us, we will have to make a stand for God. God was very specific in Psalm 1:1 as to the reason the believer is blessed. The reason the believer is blessed is because they refuse to follow advice or take council from ungodly men. And if we do not follow the pattern, it will only result in a slow but sure succession of a downward slide.

First we are enticed somewhat by what we see while passing by, and because of a continuous passing by we eventually give in and just stand around listening and seeing but not saying much, and before we know it we have totally given in to that weakness and it has become a habit, robbing us of the total victory and blessing that is ours. For example, we are facing a depression in the economy and a social life is being somewhat limited due to the lack of excess cash. Let us say after a busy and stressful week at work, your co-workers invite you to go to the mall to shop and then have dinner with them. In fact this is their every Friday after-work recreation. After many weeks of saying no and due to the extra stress you felt that week at work, you give in and agree to accompany them. Many of your co-workers are unsaved, and may not have as much financial responsibility at home like you do. While at the mall your co-workers are shopping all the latest trends and are encouraging you to do the same. You are a bit hesitant because you know your budget it already strenuous, and you refuse. But one of your co-workers decided to buy you something as a courtesy, and it made you feel appreciated, so you start lightening up. After shopping you all go to dinner and it turned out to be a nice evening. You may have gone over a little on your budget this week but it did not hurt too much. It's Friday again and now you are all excited about hanging out again. This time in the stores you are offered a credit card that could allow you to save on your first purchase. You agree because you don't want others to know you are financially strapped. At first, you purchase in small quantities but before long you are purchasing everything you like. Then you apply for credit cards at every store you frequent, and your spending has spiraled out of control. Now, as a result of trying to keep up with your co-workers, you have formed a habit that has put you in more debt.

And just like the downward spiral happens over a period of time, so, too, it will take time to reverse the process. Sometimes people can get a spectacular intervention where they are changed instantaneously, but this is an exception. God would rather we live in the supernatural, seeing his goodness and power all the time in small portions, and this is how we learn to trust him and remain in him, grounded and unshakable.

KEY #2—WE MUST FIND DELIGHT IN AND DESIRE THE WORD OF GOD

"But his delight and desire are in the law of the Lord" (Psalm 1:2a, AMP). God's intent from the very beginning was for man to operate from a position of victory and rest instead of hard, laborious work. God wanted us to enjoy what we do and he did not want us to be under bondage or commitment by force. He wanted us to choose to serve him from a position of joy and free will. Jesus's finished work at the cross has put us back to that position. In fact, Jesus invites us to give him our heavy burden as he taught his disciples to do, saying, "Take My yoke upon you and learn of Me, for I am gentle (meek) and humble (lowly) in heart, and you will find rest (relief and ease and refreshment and recreation and blessed quiet) for your souls" (Matthew 11:29, AMP).

But, because we don't know this simple truth, the enemy constantly bombards us with thinking that we still have to labor to please God, and God, somehow, is still mad at us and angry at us for our shortcomings. Instead of enjoying the Word, we go to it as a rule book for the harsh demands that God places on us to get the blessings. But nothing could be further from the truth. When Jesus moves into our heart, he equips us with everything necessary to please him. I love the way the *Message Bible* puts it: "Everything that goes into a life of pleasing God has been miraculously given to us by getting to know, personally and intimately, the One who invited us to God. The best invitation we ever received!" (2 Peter 1:3, MSG). Once this truth is established in our lives that God calls us to be in relationship with him, and then he enables us to please him. Then our mindsets will also change in the way we view God. We will not view him as demanding us, but rather equipping and enabling us to take hold of the victory that his Son died to give us. With this mindset embedded in us, we can now look to the Word with excitement and enthusiasm. We can embrace it with freedom, openness, and pleasure.

For example, an artist must first have a love and joy for his work in order to create a master piece. The difference between an artist who creates a master piece and an artist that just creates because he has to make a living is the enjoyment factor. The artist that loves and enjoys his work will be able to look at everyday sceneries that may not appear very appealing to others. But he approaches the creating process with passion and delight and as a result he is able to draw out and transform simplicity into a master piece. It is the same way with God's Word; if we look to it just because we want answers to life but we don't possess any real passion or enjoyment for the word, it would be difficult to draw out the treasures that are hidden within. And after a while when we don't realize the results we desire, our time spent in the word of God will become laborious and hard. But when we possess passion and delight for the Word of God, we will approach it with the perspective of drawing out the beauty contained within. As we meditate on God's promises, it seems as if the canvas of life comes alive with radiant colors that not only change our world but the world of others around us. It's the same way when you approach the Word of God with no hindrance and you know your heavenly father's love for you is unabated and unhindered even in your faults. You can find acceptance in him and then the Word becomes the source you desire and delight in the most.

KEY #3—HABITUAL MEDITATION

But his delight and desire are in the law of the Lord, and on His law (the precepts, the instructions, the teachings of God) he habitually meditates (ponders and studies) by day and by night.

Psalm 1:2 (AMP).

Once we have a change in perception about God—from him being angry, upset, and waiting to catch us doing wrong, to God being our father and knowing he loves us more than we can understand—then the old pattern of thinking starts to change and a new pattern is formed. Having a toned body takes exercise; we all know it does not happen with one session at the gym. The toned body is achieved through dedication and discipline to the workout routine, and over a period of time the manifestation is seen. So, too, we have to form new habits, new dedications, and new disciplines. This newfound life for the believer is the life that is lived in Christ and is dependent on his abilities to accomplish the desired results. If we depend on ourselves for the changing, it puts pressure on us and, most of the time, we tend to fail or fall short because we, being apart from our source, can't and won't be able to change anything. But, the Apostle Paul taught in the book of Philippians that we can do all things through Christ who strengthens us because we are in partnership with God, and all that we do is with his help (Philippians 4:13 AMP). I encourage you to take that first step and make a choice that could put you on the track of realizing your God-purpose. Let us decide with the help of Jesus to form new habits even as we have been allowed a second chance to do so. The fact that you are reading this book at this moment in your life should sound an alarm to you that your God-purpose is right within your grasp. Don't allow this opportunity to pass you by, thinking that maybe tomorrow or maybe next week or maybe for the New Year I will put this as one of my goals. No, my friend, I declare to you that the time is now!

THE RIGHT BELIEF SYSTEM

> For [the Spirit which] you have now received
> [is] not a spirit of slavery to put you once more
> in bondage to fear, but you have received the
> Spirit of adoption [the Spirit producing sonship]
> in [the bliss of] which we cry, Abba (Father)! Fa-
> ther! The Spirit Himself [thus] testifies together
> with our own spirit, [assuring us] that we are
> children of God.
>
> Romans 8:15-16 (AMP)

It is most important when reconstructing the mind that we always have the right mindset of who we are in Christ and not who we are in ourselves. With the right belief of being a child of the most high, the delight and desire to know him and what his plans are for us makes it easier to form the habit of meditating on his Word by day and by night.

I know what some of you are thinking, "Well, Pastor Lisa, I do have to go to work, or school, or I do have a life to live. How on earth do you expect me to meditate on Scripture day and night?" Trust me, I was faced with the same question when I was first presented with this. We are not under bondage to fear anymore and now we approach God as our Father. And as our Father, he does not want us to be afraid of him, but he wants us to see him in the capacity of that role in our lives, "Daddy" (Romans 8:15-16). Most daddies want the best for their children; no matter what they have to do to provide for them, they will do it. Well, our heavenly father has done all that he can for us already by making a way for us to be accepted by not holding back his most precious son (Jesus) from us. Through Jesus we have the acceptance as a son or daughter also. I don't want to move away from this truth too quickly because it is important that you, the believer, have the understanding of who you are in order to form the habit of meditation on God's Word.

You might say, I don't know how to meditate, but I beg to differ. I think we all know how to meditate, and, in fact, we are meditating all the time. The question to ask is, "What are we meditating on?" In order to answer this question we have to first understand what is meditation according to the Bible?

The word translated *meditate* in the English Old Testament is the Hebrew word *hagar.*

Vine's Concise Dictionary of the Bible gives this definition for the Hebrew word *hagar*—to mediate, moan, growl, utter, speak. This word means to think about something in earnest, often with the focus on thinking about future plans and contingencies, possibly speaking to God or oneself in low tones.

So, from this definition we see that mediation involves thinking and muttering. It involves the mind and the mouth. Now we can break it down even simpler; according to Psalm 1:2, God instructs us to habitually meditate on the

Law (the precepts, the instructions, and the teachings of God), which consist of the entire Bible. Since meditation consists of thinking about something earnestly and speaking in low tones, by all means you can agree with me that we all meditate by day and by night. We are always thinking about scenarios but most of the time we are thinking about everything that is happening in the present, and relating what we think on in the present to the future, thereby producing anxiety, fear, and worry. As a result of the natural and negative thought patterns, what is being produced is trickling and overflowing in the body in the form of diseases. The Apostle John prayed for us to be healthy in our souls (mind, will, and emotions) even as we are healthy in our bodies. My friends, the result of what is manifested on the outside is a clear indication of what is happening on the inside; hence, the reason God instructs us to think and ponder and speak on his Word.

POWER THOUGHTS AND CONFESSIONS

Today I will repent—I will change my mind for the better.

I desire to disconnect from the old way and embrace the new way of thinking.

I understand that my choices today will determine consequences.

I am a child of the highest God.

I desire and delight in the Word of God.

I will habitually meditate—think and ponder on, and speak the precepts, instructions, and teachings of God.

I refuse to ponder and think on my natural circumstances because my heavenly father made a perfect way for me to make it through in this life, and that is by Jesus Christ.

Everything I set out to do, I can do, because I am not empowered by my efforts but I am in Christ.

ESTABLISHING A
SOUND MIND

A I mentioned earlier, the main reason our speaking has not been effective is because our thinking is corrupted, and, as a result, we end up with little or no long-term results. I cannot stress it enough that meditation on God's Word is the foundation to a successful life. Our main focus and pursuit must be the Word of God. The main reason our lives should revolve around the Word of God is because the Word is actually our life source that feeds us, nourishes us, and causes us to become healthy in our soul. I like to call the Word of God our *soul food* and the Apostle John describes the Word this way, "[In the] beginning [before all time] was the Word (Christ), and the Word was with God, and the Word was God Himself" (John 1:1, AMP).

There should be no doubt in our minds that the Word of God is Jesus Christ, and that is why our focus is on the Word. When we read the Word of God we see Jesus in it, and when we see him we are able to see the pattern for our own lives. In order for our God-purpose to come to fruition, we must be able to maintain the mind of Christ, and as his mind is formed in us we would then be fully able to manifest his presence to the world. A constant input of the Word himself—a constant looking to Jesus and his kindness, goodness, love, and mercy toward us—will keep us in a balanced and humble place, and this place is actually where we will be able to release the life-giving Word to others that will effect change. Many of us want to affect change in the lives of others around us, but the sad reality is that change has not taken place, first, in us. Jesus faced this same scenario in his time while on the earth, so much so that he felt the need to address it. Jesus urged us to not be so consumed with trying to get the speck out of our brother's eye that we can't even see the log that is sticking out of our own eye. He wants us to first get the log out of our eyes and then try to help others (Matthew 7:3-5). The only source that can affect change in us is the Word of God. The Apostle Paul made it very clear to us that we cannot and will not be transformed unless we look and keep looking to the Word of God.

> And all of us, as with unveiled face, [because we] continued to behold [in the Word of God] as in a mirror the glory of the Lord, are constantly being transfigured into His very own image in ever increasing splendor and from one degree of glory to another; [for this comes] from the Lord [Who is] the Spirit.
>
> 2 Corinthians 3:18 (AMP)

My friends, there is no other way to be reconstructed, renewed, or transformed but by and through the Word of God.

THE WORD GIVES LIFE

"The thief comes only in order to steal and kill and destroy. I came that they may have and enjoy life, and have it in abundance (to the full, till it overflows)" (John 10:10, AMP). Our Savior is life giving, and once we are connected to him, that very same life should be flowing to us and through us to others. Everywhere Jesus went to minister he gave, he fixed, he produced, he multiplied. There was no death or negativity around him that had a chance to flourish because the God kind of life was constantly flowing. He was and still is life giving, even after he left the earth. The disciples followed in this same pattern of being a conduit of life, giving, abundance, and producing. This pattern has not changed and God has chosen the church by which to continue this flow of his life to those in need. So many times we want to preach a sermon to the world with our words, but the world will not stop and listen if there is no fruit for the world to see that what we preach is what we live. The people in the world will take notice when the believer, in spite of the down economy and depressed work place, can be positive, happy, smiling, and kind. Jesus expects us to be life giving everywhere we go, because this is the mark that we are connected to the life source. I love the fact that Jesus did not come to just give life for existence sake, but he describes it as abundant life, an overflowing life, a more than enough life, and this kind of life shows and speaks volumes to the world that he is alive and well.

The topic of Jesus Christ is inexhaustible; every which way you choose to speak about him, the end result is beautiful. He always had time to stop and heal the sick, feed the multitudes, deliver the demon-possessed and oppressed. He had time to stop and hug the children, bring the dead back to life, and teach his disciples while maintaining his composure; even unto death he still exuded life. This sure sounds like an abundant life to me. No matter how full his schedule was there was always enough grace surrounding him to get it done, and this is the very same life he came to give us. It always amazes me that the awesome God we serve did not ask us to operate by a standard that he himself did not follow. He is not harsh in his requirements, but in actuality he leads by example that it could be done. And he does not stop there, he offers us his Holy Spirit to help us. What an awesome God we serve, and gaining this revelation of the life that flows from him is enough to energize our faith and enable us to keep steadfastly pursuing the abundant life.

BACK TO THE BASICS

The reason this most powerful key of Bible mediation is bypassed so often is because many of us think it is way too simple, and, as a result, we are always reaching for something more complex. I truly believe we need to get back to the basics where the simple truths of God's Word become the priority in establishing the believer on their God-purpose. We cannot continue to put the cart before the horse. In the same way, we need to get back to teaching the body of Christ how to become healthy while they are growing in God. I am in no way disputing the need to teach sound doctrine and good theology, because the Apostle Paul majored in sound doctrine to the churches in the New Testament, but not before he established them in the grace and love of Jesus Christ.

His first priority was to make sure that the finished work of Jesus Christ was never under played by the old covenant (the law). So then, the basics of the cross, justification only by the blood of Jesus Christ, redemption from slavery to sin and death, the power of Christ and his resurrection, was the Apostle Paul's priority. And these are the basics that need to be taught to the believers again. But when the believer is not equipped with the basics of how to bring that seed of Christ, which is deposited in them at the new birth to fruition, then we will continually have babes in the house of God, always needing a crutch to walk on, always needing an emotional fix, always needing the leader to pray and lay hands on us instead of us being able to do those very said things for others. If we are ever going to walk in the abundant life that Jesus came to give us, then the basics of his Word must now become the priority in our lives. In order to establish a sound mind we must have a constant, inward flow of the anointed Word of God revolving in our minds and mouths. It is my prayer that this key will change your lives forever, and that the mind of Christ be formed in you as you venture to take this new path in your life.

CHEWING ON SCRIPTURE

"Instead, you thrill to God's Word, you chew on Scripture day and night" (Psalm 1:2, MSG). I love the use of the word "chew" in the *Message* translation of Psalm 1:2. I mentioned earlier that the law of the Lord consists of the whole Bible, and, of course, we cannot learn the whole Bible by heart for success. So how do we as believers go about this process? Do we literally take a bite out of the Bible and start chewing the pages? Of course not! I would like to help you through the process of Bible meditation and the beauty that evolves in the soul from chewing on Scriptures. It is one thing to memorize the Bible, and it helps in meditation, but it is not the full process of Bible mediation. Sometimes we can be over enthusiastic and decide we are going to read the whole Bible from beginning to end in one year. Of course, I have no problem with that resolution if that is your heart's desire, but to meditate God's way means it will take more than a year; in fact, it will take you your whole lifetime. And because we have the spirit of God dwelling on the inside of us, he would lead us always to the Scriptures we will need to meditate on for the specific times we may be facing in our lives. I will share a few basic steps and examples on Bible mediation or the chewing of Scripture.

SET ASIDE TIME ON PURPOSE

Specific daily times of devotions are a great way to establish your Bible mediation. It is imperative that we teach believers the importance of establishing a relationship with Jesus for themselves. There are many wonderful tools and resources to help the believer grow today with the fast and ever up-grading of the technology world. While many of these tools and resources are great, it should really just add to our relationship with God and not be the only source of nourishment for us. God desires to communicate with each of us individually and on a personal level, and this is accomplished by us taking up his Word on purpose and finding out who he is for ourselves. Because we are now living our lives with the help of the Holy Spirit, he knows what the God-purpose is for our lives, and he will show us this plan through the Word of God.

God likes to speak to us corporately when we go to church, but he also loves to speak to his children through his Word in intimate moments with them as they search out his words. I would suggest you start off with small portions of Scripture for your reading and use a translation that makes it easy to understand. Personally, I use the *Amplified Bible*, the *Message Bible*, and the *New King James* version. Before you read the Word, pray and ask God to make the Scriptures clear to you. Let us use an example of Psalm 23; it only has six verses, yet when you sit to read it with the intention of finding food and nourishment for your soul, you will find that you can spend days chewing on this scripture and keep finding strength in it. I would suggest one verse at a time and prepare yourself with a pen and notepad to make notes of the things you find life giving.

Example of Bible Meditation

Remember, to meditate means to ponder and think about and then mutter under your breath or in low tones. Now, keeping this in mind, you can start your meditation for the day. I would strongly suggest taking this one Psalm as your focus for the whole week. Read the whole Psalm once and then go verse by verse—one verse per day. I have noticed that asking questions and answering these questions based on earthly examples brings a clear picture of the verse to mind. It was also the pattern of Jesus's teaching style. He would always use examples of trees, farmers, sheep, etc. He used simple, everyday examples of creation to explain the kingdom so that everyday people like you and me could understand it. So let's get started!

DAY 1

[The Lord] is my Shepherd [to feed, guide, and shield me], I shall not lack

Psalm 23:1 (AMP)

Q. What is this verse saying?

A. The Lord is my Shepherd

Q. Who is the Lord?

A. Jesus Christ is my Lord and he is the Creator of this universe—he holds it in his hands; not only that, but he left his home on high and came to this earth and paid the price for me to be accepted by God the Father—he is the Lord.

Q. What does a shepherd do?

A. A shepherd leads and is responsible for his sheep; therefore, he has to walk with them, guide them, look over them, feed them, and protect them from danger.

SUMMARY

The Creator of this universe, who holds everything in place, is also the one responsible to walk, guide, look over, provide, and protect me, and because he is my shepherd I shall not lack in any area.

PRACTICAL APPLICATION

Now you have a set Scripture before you; you have thought about it and have some answers to dwell on. But how do you keep mediating when you have to go to work and be around people, answer the phones, work on excel reports, meet with clients, or go to meetings? Trust me, God knows you have to live and go about your daily lives, but now, because you have equipped your mind with the Word of God, as you leave the house to get to work you have some time on your hands in the transportation process. Maybe on the bus, train, taxi, or driving your car, you can actually use the time to ponder the notes you made during your devotion time. And while you are pondering and thinking, you can speak to yourself by asking the same questions you asked earlier and answering them the same way. But now you are actually using your mouth to mutter the question and answer process. Muttering does not involve loud speaking—it is in very low tones, or you can even go through the process in your mind just rolling around the scripture, "The Lord is my Shepherd and I shall not lack."

As your day progresses, you will have a lunch or tea break and, again, it is an opportunity to meditate. You have the journey back home from work and, again, it is another opportunity for meditation. Finally, before you go to bed you can choose to take time to focus on that one verse again, instead of sitting and watching a scary movie that may cause your mind to enter into a state of disarray before you sleep. I guarantee you this meditation may even invoke the best sleep you ever had, simply because you are thinking on God thoughts for your life. You see, the misconception is that we should read a whole portion for just reading the Bible sake, but at the end of the week, nothing sticks with us and we are back to the drawing board of frustration—both with ourselves and with God. But, I can assure you, this way is God's way, and we build and grow precept upon precept, thereby building a strong foundation, which, over a period of time, will not be easily shaken by the pressures of everyday life. Now, following the same pattern, I have done it for the rest of the verses for Psalm 23.

DAY 2

He makes me lie down in [fresh, tender] green pastures; He leads me beside the still and restful waters.

Psalm 23:2 (AMP)

A. Green gives the picture of freshness, lushness, and full of nutrients; and pastures talks about big open space as in the idea of abundance. Also, the verse does not say *pasture,* as in one, but *pastures,* as in many—over abundance. In reference to the sheep, this talks about supply of food and natural sustenance.

Q. Do I have to find still and restful waters?

A. No, the verse says that he leads me, so the shepherd himself will bring me to this place once I am following him.

Q. What is still and restful waters?

A. It gives the picture of a stream that is flowing, yet very peaceful, that I can drink and quench my thirst and still sit down and rest. It is not loud and does not consist of big crashing waves causing fear, chaos, and confusion. There is the existence of peace, and this peace comes from knowing that the shepherd is still looking over me, even while I enjoy the blessings he leads me to.

SUMMARY

The Lord is my shepherd, and He is responsible for me. He will provide all my natural needs of food and drink, in abundance, and, at the same time, I will be able to find physical rest and restoration.

DAY 3

He refreshes and restores my life (myself); He leads me in the paths of righteousness [uprightness and right standing with Him—not for my earning it, but] for His name's sake.

Psalm 23:3 (AMP).

Q. What does the shepherd do for me?

A. Because of what Jesus did at the cross, in spite of the harshness of the natural circumstances I face right now, I will be able to find restoration and peace of mind in Christ and his finished work at the cross.

Q. Where does he lead me today?

A. The shepherd, who also is the Word, is showing me that the right standing that I desire with him does not come through anything I can do or any of my human efforts, but, rather, it is free in him and only through his name. My Shepherd knows the beaten tracks of life, and because he walked this very same road, I can rest assured that he is leading me in the right direction.

SUMMARY

My right standing with the shepherd today does not come through my works or efforts. I am made righteous, and I find acceptance because of the shepherd himself and what he accomplished through his death, burial, and resurrection. I am accepted, and a way is being made for me, solely on the shepherd's qualifications and not my own.

DAY 4

Yes, though I walk through the [deep, sunless] valley of the shadow of death, I will fear or dread no evil, for You are with me; Your rod [to protect] and Your staff [to guide], they comfort me.

Psalm 23:4 (AMP)

Q. Does the Lord lead me to the valley of death?

A. No, sometimes in my life I may make wrong decisions that may cause me to come off the track that the shepherd is leading me on. Sometimes, I may get distracted by the glamour of the world, and, as a result, I may end up in difficult situations, but I remember somewhere else in the Bible it says that the Lord is with me and he will never leave me. So, even in this time of unsightly circumstances, the shepherd will be there with his Word to bring me back on track if I call on him. And when I come back on the paths he has for me, he will welcome and comfort me.

SUMMARY

The Lord, who is my shepherd, is with me and I know even if I fail as a result of my own choice, when I repent, he will not condemn me.

DAY 5

You prepare a table before me in the presence of my enemies. You anoint my head with oil; my [brimming] cup runs over.

Psalm 23:5 (AMP)

Q. What does preparing a table in the presence of my enemies mean?

A. The enemy always wants the children of God to be crushed because he hates everything about the shepherd, and usually his way of getting to me is by using other people to work against me. But, if I continue to let the shepherd lead my life, he will cause everything I do to prosper, and those around me that are trying to hurt me will not be able to deny that the Lord is with me.

Q. What does anointing my head with oil mean?

A. In the morning before the shepherd would take the sheep out, it is told that he would put oil on their head and it would run down to the rest of the body in the event that the sheep gets hurt, then the oil would soothe and protect the cut or bruise from being infected and also keep the flies away. In the same way, my shepherd gives me the Holy Spirit today and he is my anointing to protect me from the wiles of the enemy.

SUMMARY

Today I have the Holy Spirit and he anoints me with his power so that no weapon formed against me shall prosper, and in spite of the efforts of the enemy to pull me down, my shepherd will allow me to remain in peace and wholeness.

DAY 6

Surely or only goodness, mercy, and unfailing love shall follow me all the days of my life, and through the length of my days the house of the

Lord [and His presence] shall be my dwelling place.

Psalm 23:6 (AMP)

Q. What will follow me?

A. In order for something to follow me I must be moving forward. And I am being led by my shepherd and my shepherd is the Lord of this universe. Therefore, he is constantly leading me on a path that leads to him. Once I remain on that path, goodness and mercy will follow me. And the verse does not say maybe but surely goodness and mercy will follow me.

Q. How long will goodness and mercy follow me?

A. All the days of my life.

Q. Where will my dwelling place be?

A. My dwelling place is in the shepherd's presence, and in his presence I know I will be safe.

SUMMARY

The Shepherd will lead me and surely goodness and mercy will back me up and, as a result, my daily life will constantly be spent in the presence of my Lord. With the Lord surrounding me like this, it is impossible to fail today!

Congratulations! You have completed one week of Bible meditation; you have more in your soul in one week as opposed to randomly reading the Bible and going along your merry way. You have started to build a consistent foundation that would stand in any crisis or the worst of conditions. This pattern for Bible meditation not only leads to a sound mind, but it ignites hope (a confident, joyful expectation of good), even in bad situations and circumstances. This simple, yet very effective pattern can and will apply to all your Bible reading from hence forth; it is not complicated. Bible mediation is a very effective principle and if we could grasp that the only source we can have confidence in is God's Word, then we would truly lead the lives that God intended us to live, and that is the abundant life.

POWER THOUGHTS
AND CONFESSIONS

I am in the process of establishing a sound mind.

Jesus is the Word of God and I look to him to be transformed.

The Word (Jesus) gives me the abundant life.

I choose to ponder and chew on Scripture.

I choose to set aside time on purpose to meditate on God's Word.

The Lord is my shepherd and because he is my shepherd I will not lack anything; I will be protected; I will have rest and refreshment; and I will have peace.

Today, the Lord goes before me, and surely goodness and mercy is following me; therefore, I will dwell in his presence constantly.

I am determined to make Bible meditation a priority in my daily walk.

The Benefits of Consistent Bible Mediation

In everyday life we are faced with many problems and having confidence in the Word of God is the weapon that we need to combat these issues. Having been equipped with the tool of Bible meditation, you will be able to see the practical application come to the forefront when faced with trials, troubles, pressures, and tribulations. The Apostle Paul stated it this way, "God's Word is an indispensable weapon" (Ephesians 6:15, MSG).

After a few weeks or months of meditating this way, your mind is now becoming saturated with the words that God has spoken for your life as opposed to the negatives you may have heard your whole life. Some of the words that would be revolving in your mind are words like: moving forward, progression, healing, freedom, wholeness, satisfaction, more than enough, joyful, peace, and abundance. This condition of your mind is sound and stable and will continue to become stronger and stronger as you keep following the process of Bible mediation. And what you are really doing by renewing your mind with the Word of God is in actuality causing your soul to be equipped to deal with any difficult problem or situation that may arise. Now you are not spending time on wishing away the problems or worrying about the problems, but you are strengthening yourself to have confidence in your God who is able to help you deal with it all.

Let us examine a practical scenario of how Bible meditation, when established in the believer's life, would operate. Let us use the work place as an example; the business you work for is cutting back because of the downturn in the economy and all the employees are going to be effected by this. In a time when everyone around starts panicking and getting anxious, you will be able to stay calm and focused, and remain in peace because of your consistent mediation on the Word of God and his promises to you. The Holy Spirit will now bring back the promises necessary to help strengthen and establish you in the time of despair. He may bring back that verse from Psalm 23, "The Lord is my shepherd, I shall not lack," and as it comes to your mind, immediately the fear you might feel as a result of the pay cut will suddenly dissipate and be replaced by God's peace.

I can assure you that over a period of time when you practice Bible meditation, confidence is built in the Lord and his abilities to see you through. This is a foundation that will prove to be sure and strong. We will continue to face many trails while on this earth, and there will be times when our pastors and leaders won't be so easily accessible. Where would that leave us? We have to be able to know and have confidence in the one that is accessible, that even when we are sleeping, he is working on our behalf, and his name is Faithful and True. We must come to a point where we understand that knowing this truth only comes through knowing his Word, and knowing his Word comes with the help of the Holy Spirit by means of Bible meditation.

WHAT ARE THE BENEFITS OF CONSISTENT BIBLE MEDITATION?

> And he shall be like a tree firmly planted [and tended] by the streams of water, ready to bring forth its fruit in its season; its leaf also shall not fade or wither; and everything he does shall prosper [and come to maturity].
>
> Psalm 1:3 (AMP)

1) THE BELIEVER WILL BE FIRMLY PLANTED

The Lord goes on to describe the person who meditates on his Word according to his way, as a tree firmly planted by the streams of water. God uses the examples from creation like trees, birds, fish, and sheep, and he relates it to, everyday life. He uses these examples of creation, and he draws analogies to us and our lives, in order for us to grasp the wealth of his wisdom in its entire splendor, without it being so complicated. The scripture above has a wealth of wisdom in it. It states very clearly that the person that chews on Scripture (Bible meditation), as described in the previous chapter, will become established, abounding, unshakable, and firm.

Take a look around you. There are many trees everywhere and they look beautiful and strong. Some trees just grow wild without much attention for years, while some are planted in gardens, and these are taken care of often through pruning and watering. But the real test of character for these trees would be determined by their ability to remain standing after the storms and hurricanes pass through.

When we think about being firmly planted, we think about roots digging deep into the soil, and the further down the roots go, the more likely the tree will be able to hold on in the midst of the high storms and strong winds. As the roots go down deep, they are able to take in all the rich nutrients and all the goodness from the soil, and then the nutrients travel through the roots to the rest of the tree, producing a strong, stable, and healthy tree. So the tree is only as strong as its roots. In essence, the soil here would be the Word of God, and the roots would be the soul (the mind, will, and emotions); and when the soul meditates on the Word of God, the soul is nourished and grows in God's ways, thereby retaining the ability to remain strong in the midst of and after the storm. God is saying that the believer that ponders and thinks about his instructions and teachings and speaks them continually will be like that tree that is firmly planted, and when it is hit with the storms, the wind currents, and the tornadoes of life, they will remain strong, immovable, and grounded.

2) THE BELIEVER WILL HAVE AN ABUNDANT SUPPLY AND REFRESHING FOR THE SOUL

The tree that the Lord describes will not only be planted firmly but it will be planted by streams of water. God will supply abundantly for the believer who makes the Word his focus and his food. Water also gives us the feeling of refreshment and when someone is refreshed it means that they have had time to rest. Our rest is in Christ, and that is why Jesus cried out on the cross, "It is finished" (John 19:30, AMP). So when we ponder and chew on Scripture, like, "I have received the gift of righteousness and abundant grace" (Romans 5:17 AMP), this causes us to rest in Christ's finished work. It opens up our understanding to the truth that we don't have to work hard or fight for right standing with God because it is a gift and it is free.

As we choose to think about God's grace toward us and how our faults and shortcomings are all covered by the blood of the lamb, we can find rest and refreshing for our souls, inner peace and calmness. It is the constant keeping of our roots in the soil that contains the water that washes over our souls and produces the ability to remove the clutter and junk that causes sickness and disease in our bodies. The streams of water purify our souls by removing toxic and impure thoughts that could hinder our production process. The streams of water are also moving, and moving water is considered living water. When the believer ponders on and speaks the words of God, the living water, or moving water, will remove anything that could cause a blockage and that would ultimately cause the believer to become contaminated or stagnant in their walk with God. We truly do need the abundance of the streams of water to help sustain and maintain a prosperous soul.

3) THE BELIEVER SHALL PRODUCE OUT OF REST

The process that takes place in one verse that can transform our lives if we grasp it wholeheartedly is just amazing. The believer that ponders and chews on Scripture is also described as ready to bring forth fruit in its season. This gives the idea of being productive and having the ability to create—but not only create for creating sake, but create or produce with the purpose to be of use to someone else—the God-purpose. In reality, the reason we are blessed is, in turn, to become a blessing. What good is it if we have all the success in the world but cannot speak a kind word to another human being? Or what is the use to have to work seven days a week and not have time to enjoy the wealth with our families? This is much of the world system, and God does not want us to operate under this system of producing through stress; he wants us to produce by his system, which is through rest and enjoyment. In Dr. Caroline Leaf's book, *Who Switched off My Brain*, she states,

> If you don't build relaxation into your lifestyle you will become a less effective thinker, defeating your ability to accomplish the mental tasks that stole your relaxation in the first place. In fact, for the brain to function like it should, it needs regroup/consolidation time. If it doesn't get this, it will send out signals in the form of high-level stress hormones, some of which are epinephrine, norepinephrine and cortisol. If these chemicals constantly flow, they create a "white noise" effect that increase anxiety and blocks clear thinking and the processing of information" (144–145)

When I think on the creation of the earth in the first chapter of Genesis, nowhere do I find God upset, disgruntled, or frustrated in his creating process. Everything he created he was happy with. Not only that, but God did not create the earth for himself to enjoy, he created it for us to be blessed by his blessings.

We also see that the production or creativity is in a season, and that describes the ability to wait on God's timing and not rush ahead. God has a specific and appointed time for everything, and, most times, many of the problems we encounter are due to our inability to wait on the appointed time. We live in a society where everything has to happen now—the faster the better. Internet service carriers are all focused on how to increase speed. Gone are the days when we take the family on a shopping day and spend quality time together; now, all we have to do is open up the browser and the shopping world is at our fingertips. While this may provide convenience, we are losing moments of precious conversations with our spouses and children; we hardly know what our neighbors look like because we are always on a very fast-pace schedule.

This is not God's plan for the producing and creating process for the believer's life. God does not want us moving at roadrunner speed; he wants us to operate within the purpose we were created for. He wants us to operate out of rest and refreshment. In order to move away from the fast pace society we live in, we must maintain a life that is surrounded by meditating on the Word of God. As we continue to do this, our focus will shift from our producing, and our end result will take us to the source—which is Jesus Christ; and because of the shift in focus, we will be able to produce without much self-effort, all in the right time. God wants us to be able to produce and create from a place of us resting in him and his abilities, which will always bring quality to our lives.

4) THE BELIEVER SHALL PROSPER IN THEIR GOD-PURPOSE

As the believer ponders and speaks God's Word, it states that the believer will prosper in everything they do (Psalm 1:3

AMP). Keep in mind this everything is tied in to the context of God's word and his ways for your expected end. Remember, Bible meditation transforms us and brings us into alignment with God's plan for our lives. The Apostle Paul says it this way,

> And all of us, as with unveiled face, [because we] continued to behold [in the Word of God] as in a mirror the glory of the Lord, are constantly being transfigured into His *very own* image in ever increasing splendor *and* from one degree of glory to another; [for this comes] from the Lord [Who is] the Spirit.
>
> 2 Corinthians 3:18 (AMP)

As we continue to meditate on God's word, we will most definitely be transformed into his image. And as that transformation takes place, we will walk out our God-purpose. By all means, almost every person has a desire to be prosperous, but not everyone wants to acquire it God's way. But, God's way of consistent Bible meditation will produce lasting results.

To prosper gives the idea of reaching the point of success, or to be successful. And maturity gives the idea of something constantly growing until it reaches the point of producing more. You do not get the idea of a quitter that starts a project and then leaves it unfinished and moves on to another project. The believer who is meditating on God's Word will have clarity on their God-purpose, then they will stay with that God-purpose until it comes to fruition.

I am reminded of the story of Joseph in the book of Genesis when he was sold into slavery and ended up in Potiphar's house. The one thing that caused Joseph to be elevated to the highest position available was the visible evidence his master saw, and that evidence was that everything he put his hands to was prospering; it was thriving and becoming successful. This brings us to the purpose of our prosperity and that is so the people around us can see the God we serve at work in our lives. Joseph did not wait until he was promoted to show off his skills; he took the menial everyday grind of the job and gave his best. He gave thanks for what he had and where he was, and because of this thankful heart and the promise of his God, he was able to prosper. Bible meditation releases us from the stronghold of the quitter's perspective, and unlocks the vault of God's endless resources to make us prosperous and bring everything we do to full maturity. Meditation on God's Word, with the help of the Holy Spirit, is our guarantee to the God-purpose life. In fact, it is the crux or very foundation of our faith. Mediation on God's Word is based on his promises, and his promises are based on truth. The author of the book of Hebrews says it this way, "Let's keep a firm grip on the promises that keep us going. He always keeps his word" (Hebrews 10:23, MSG).

> [Most] blessed is the man who believes in, trusts in, and relies on the Lord, and whose hope and confidence the Lord is. For he shall be like a tree

planted by the waters that spreads out its roots by the river; and it shall not see and fear when heat comes; but its leaf shall be green. It shall not be anxious and full of care in the year of drought, nor shall it cease yielding fruit.

Jeremiah 17:7-8 (AMP)

We truly cannot arrive to the point of trusting God, relying on God, and having confidence in God if we do not know him and his character. The whole purpose of this book is to bring you, the believer, into a closer and more intimate relationship with your heavenly father by beholding his Son, with the help of the Holy Spirit. The only way to the Father's heart is through his Son, and no one knows the Son better than the spirit of God. God wrote the Book to reveal to us his love, his plan, and his intentions for us, but it is up to us to search out his promises and make them ours. The ultimate way to accomplish this is through meditation on God's Word, pondering on the truths of God and then giving those truths power as we speak them in faith. Then and only then can we be like that tree planted by the streams of water, having our roots go down deep, becoming strong with power to endure the hardships of this life and still be able to produce life to help others in need of our Savior!

POWER THOUGHTS
AND CONFESSIONS

I will reap the benefits of consistent Bible meditation.

God's Word is an indispensable weapon in my life.

I will be like a tree firmly planted by streams of water.

I will constantly have an abundant supply of the God-life flowing through me.

I will produce out of rest in Christ.

Everything I put my hands to will prosper and come to maturity.

Today I am not a quitter but a winner in Christ.

I will be blessed so that I can be a blessing.

GOOD SUCCESS

Almost everyone in this world wants to be successful, and by the world system, many appear to be. But, according to God's Word, success is referred to as "good success" (Joshua 1:8 AMP). It is God's will that the believer come into good success and not just success. Most of the time, we measure success in terms of material possessions. While this might be true according to the world's definition of success, in God's definition it is not the entire truth. No one gets up in the morning and declares, "I wonder how I can fail today?" Every one of us wants the taste of success, and we live our whole lives chasing success as the world presents it. Success, the world's way, is packaged nicely on the outside. The trimmings and bows on a package may make it look enticing, but the contents may not match up to that which is on the outside. In the same way when we chase after success the world's way, we end up only chasing the appearance of something beautiful on the outside, but the inside is empty. In reality, this success is on a very superficial level and will constantly demand all our efforts and energies to sustain it. And even though this pattern of success may bring us many material possessions, such as multiple cars, several houses, swimming pools, personal gyms, entertainment centers, a private beach, social networking with the rich and famous, walking the red carpet, and a continuous spot light, it also does a great job at hiding the other results attained while getting the *possessions* we desire. Many rich and famous people ended up taking their own lives because the reality of the success package was way too much for them to handle. The pressures of maintaining the lime light demanded a rigorous social life, such as, continuous public appearances and performances, clubbing and partying. And in order to keep their energy level up they would have to depend on drugs for support. After a while the occasional use becomes a habit and eventually turns into drug abuse. Even though they possessed all that money could buy, they still lacked true happiness. Perhaps it is the realization of the emptiness of their success package when it is unwrapped that causes them to give up hope and tragically end it all.

In these very difficult and trying times of a downturn in the economy, which is affecting everyone on every level, success does not even seem like a possibility in our vocabulary anymore. In this time, what we need is a revelation of the God we serve and his set pattern for our good success. The Apostle Paul said it this way, "If we are faithless [do not believe and are untrue to Him], He remains true (faithful to His Word and His righteous character), for He cannot deny Himself" (2 Timothy 2:13, AMP).

REVELATION

This is the foundation we need to build our future on. Our future cannot be built on the world system; it must be built on the revelation of the God who holds everything in his hands. Well, you might say that you are using the principles of God and are still not seeing any progress. This is because we are using the principles without a revelation of the *one* who gave the principles. But when God's principles are used with a revelation of him, then what we do will remain and not crumble in spite of a downturn in the economy. God's way includes a relationship with him, which really is more valuable than success itself. When we take time to ponder this concept we will realize that good success is a byproduct of the relationship we have with our heavenly Father.

We don't need another system and we don't need more information that is empty and void of power. What we do need is a revelation of the one who wrote the handbook. Let's explore for a moment: When you are making a decision to purchase something of value or thinking about investing for your future, what is the first thing you look at or look for? Do you look at the handbook first? No, the first thing most people look for is the brand name. And once the name of the company is reputable; then you invest. For example, if you are about to invest in a computer for home use you would research the best brand on the market. Once you have enough information on the most reputable name in the industry you will invest in your computer. Once you purchase the computer, then you receive the handbook or the manual of how to operate the computer.

The believer must follow the same pattern. We must know the God we serve has the name above all names, and he does not produce or create anything cheap, inferior, or destined to fail. Once we know our God, then the handbook, which is his Word, leads us in the direction of how to operate and remain in good success. Good success, according to God's way, is not here today and gone tomorrow. Good success, according to God's way, does not and is not effected by the world system. When God gives good success, nothing and no one in the natural will be able to shake it, pull it down, or destroy it because the master's hand is upon it. In all of our acquiring, may our prayer be to acquire revelation of the Creator himself.

GOOD SUCCESS ACCORDING TO GOD'S PATTERN CONTAINS A PLAN, PROMISE, AND INSTRUCTIONS

God is very precise about the plans and purposes for our lives, just as he was with the men and women in the Bible. God was clear to Abraham that he was to leave his father's land and go to a place where he would lead him and make of him a great nation. God led Moses into the desert so he could give him the plan that would set millions of his children out of bondage into freedom. No one ventures into something new without a plan because that would only breathe an environment of chaos and confusion, and where there is chaos and confusion, there is failure. But a God-plan gives birth to a God-vision, and a God-vision fuels the God-purpose for our lives. In other words, we cannot function or reach our God-purpose without a God-plan.

I would like us to examine the life of Joshua who experienced good success, and I earnestly desire for you to be able to see and grasp the pattern he followed according to God's word in order to attain the result of the God-purpose intended for him. Joshua was a man of great knowledge and experience because he spent many years working right alongside one of the greatest generals in his time, Moses. Joshua was familiar with God's ways, God's heart, and God's love for his people. He was faithful in his service both to Moses and God, and though his fellow men doubted God, he understood that God had a plan and a purpose for him and the children of Israel. He knew that in order to accomplish the great feat set before him, it would require a God-plan, and he needed to possess the presence of God with him every step of the way. Let us take a closer look at the pattern of success that Joshua followed as instructed by God.

THE PLAN

[After the] death of Moses the servant of the Lord, the Lord said to Joshua son of Nun, Moses' minister, Moses My servant is dead. So now arise [take his place], go over this Jordan, you and all this people, into the land which I am giving to them, the Israelites.

Joshua 1:1-2 (AMP)

In the verses above we can see that God was very clear about the purpose for Joshua's life. God lays out the plan with no misunderstandings, no guessing, no trial and error, and no maybe so, hope so, or someday so. Many times there seems to be a misunderstanding in the body of Christ that God's plan is not really clear. Or sometimes we believe unless we make right every wrong from our past and reverse every generational curse, we will never be able to see the plan of God unfold in our lives. As a result of these misconceptions, many believers fall by the way side without ever realizing their God-purpose. They realized it would be a never-ending process to fix all the wrongs from the past, and break every curse, so they end up spending a lifetime wandering in the wilderness of this harsh world. Instead of the Lord telling Joshua to look back at his past, the Lord encourages him to look forward in spite of his loss, pains, and fears. God's purpose for us is very clear, and he does not want us to get over occupied about what we have done in the past or what we have lost. This is the enemy's tactic and he loves it when we sit down and wallow in our loss, failures, and shortcomings because this is the thinking pattern that will cripple us and keep us from embracing the God-plan for our God-purpose.

Joshua experienced a major loss in his life. The leader of all leaders, in his eyes, was gone and the mantle was now upon his shoulders. He did not stay longer than necessary to mourn the great loss. Sometimes we cannot take hold of the plan because we are still mourning over a loss such as a divorce or failure in business. We are mourning over our dad walking out on us when we were kids, or mourning over a life of abuses. All of these issues are real and they do happen, but when we mourn longer than we should, we create an obstacle that keeps us from moving forward into the plan God has for us. We have to do what God told Joshua to do, "Face the reality that Moses is dead now. You had sufficient time to mourn his loss and now it's time to move into full gear and walk out your God-purpose" (Joshua 1:2 AMP).

As long as we remain occupied with the loss, we will not be able to have clarity of vision to see the God-plan. I hope to clear up these misunderstandings, and I want to reassure you with great resolve and conviction of heart that the God you serve is very interested in making his plans and purposes very clear to you!

THE PROMISE

Every place upon which the sole of your foot shall tread, that have I given to you, as I promised Moses. From the wilderness and this Lebanon to the great river Euphrates—all the land of the Hittites [Canaan]—and to the Great [Mediterranean] Sea on the west shall be your territory. No man shall be able to stand before you all the days of your life. As I was with Moses, so I will be with you; I will not fail you or forsake you.

Joshua 1:3-5 (AMP)

The plan of God for your life will always be supported with his promise. What good would it be if we had a plan but no promise to back it up? Our God was, is, and always will be the God of his Word; he is a covenant-keeping God—it is who he is and he cannot go against it. This is why God did not cut a covenant with man, because he knows man will never be able to keep that covenant. Instead, he made a covenant with God the Son—the covenant or promise was cut in his blood and not our own, sealing that covenant with himself. God could do this because he is able to keep his Word until the end of the age, and his Word is the foundation and life of our very being.

Too many times we continue to base our future on empty promises made by men who hold a position in society. For example, on the work place we may be promised a promotion by the boss if we can increase sales for the company. Then three months later someone more qualified comes along and we are forgotten. And at the end of it all, it was all based on an illusion that leads to a dead end. I want to encourage you to take God at his Word, because his Word tells us that everything will pass away but not one dot from his Word will pass away, and this, my friends, is a promise beyond promises (Matthew 24:35 AMP).

I often take time out to ponder the simple reasoning's of life, like what kind of parents would tell their child, "We have a plan for you; it is for you to get a great education, and once you attain this education you will be assured of a good position in life." And after the parents give the child the plan for success, the parents abandon the child. Now the child is left alone to find all the resources necessary for a great education without any further help or guidance from the parents. God will back up the plan he has for your life with his Word, which is his promise. Failure is often the result in man using the promises of men to fulfill the God-plan for our lives. But a God-plan will always require a God-promise and not a man-promise!

With the promise of God, Joshua was enabled and empowered to accomplish his God-purpose. The promise of God somehow seems to fuel us to keep moving forward because with the God-promise we know we are working toward a productive end, even in times when we may feel like giving up. The promise is very vital to us finishing with joy, and it also causes us to work with purpose. The promise crystallizes the God-purpose, and when the future becomes hazy, we always have God's promise to rely on for strength and hope.

THE INSTRUCTIONS

This book of the Law shall not depart out of your mouth, but you shall meditate on it day and night, that you may observe and do according to all that is written in it. For then you shall make your way prosperous, and then you shall deal wisely and have good success.

Joshua 1:8 (AMP)

After God lays out the plan and equips us with the promise, he will most definitely give us the instructions to make that plan a success. You see, God has done all he can to give you the life he intended for you. But the fact remains that you have to do your part. You must possess the promise, which you have to make yours. For the new covenant believer, the work was already done over two thousand years ago on Calvary's hill. God sent his Son to take our place of sin, sickness, poverty, and shame so we could receive righteousness, health, prosperity, peace of mind, and victory. Therefore, possessing the promise is made so much easier for us if we would learn how to remain in Christ. One might think that Joshua going forth to possess the land would require a lot of natural fighting skills, great strategies of war planning, having an army that has never lost a battle, and having a barrage of powerful weapons in his arsenal, but God's instructions to Joshua required God's abilities more than Joshua's abilities. The key to possessing our promise is really remaining confident in his ability to bring it to pass, as opposed to our own abilities. On more than one occasion, God urged Joshua not to be afraid. When our confidence shifts from God and his abilities, to us and our inabilities, it is very easy to become fearful. The plan that God has for you is a big one that will require him. If the plan is small and you can handle it, then why would there be a need for him in the first place. God plans in grandeur for his children, so the less of us there is, the more of him there will be.

If the key to being prosperous is to remain confident in God's abilities to bring the promise to pass then the question remains, how do we remain confident in his abilities? The answer lies in verse 8 of Joshua, chapter 1.

> This book of the Law shall not depart out of your mouth, but you shall meditate on it day and night, that you may observe and do according to all that is written in it. For then you shall make your way prosperous, and then you shall deal wisely and have good success.
>
> Joshua 1:8 (AMP)

The Lord instructed Joshua that the book of the law shall not depart from his mouth and that he should mediate on it day and night. It is the same principle we talked about in Psalm 1.

And what is more interesting is that the same Hebrew word used in Psalm 1 for meditate (hagar) is the same word used here in Joshua 1:8. God did not instruct Joshua to go into six months of intense physical training, and neither did he say, "Enter into boot camp." But the instruction was to get the Word on the inside of him. In order to remain confident in God's abilities to bring the promises to pass, we have to focus, ponder, think about, and speak the promises. This principle was laid down from very early on in God's Word and it has not changed. It is we who are changing because of the inability to maintain consistency in right believing. Somehow man's opinions and thoughts and strategies seem to take the forefront and God's Word and promises become the last resort in the backup plan. Sometimes, unless we exhaust all our resources and truly come to the end of ourselves, we will not truly be able to embrace God and his Word as the priority in our lives. My friends, I want to encourage you to take God's instruction first in your life, and I assure you that the results of good success will most definitely manifest!

POWER THOUGHTS
AND CONFESSIONS

I am not interested in success, but I will experience good success.

I will follow the God-pattern for good success.

I thank you, Lord, for the revelation of your Word.

I will live my life by revelation and not information.

I thank you, Lord, that success your way includes a plan, a promise, and a set of instructions.

I will embrace the God-plan for my life.

I will stand on the promises of God today and not the opinions of man.

I choose to use the instructions of Bible meditation to accomplish good success.

THE POWER OF
THE SPOKEN WORD

The New Covenant believer's work is to believe and speak, and we have covered the aspect of believing. Now we want to venture into the aspect of speaking. Once our thinking is lined up with the plans, purposes, and promises of God, the speaking aspect becomes effective automatically. Earlier I said that God had spoken to me, and He said, "Your speaking is ineffective because your thinking is corrupted."

Once our thinking is straightened out, our speaking becomes the avenue by which the blessings will be able to manifest in the natural. The blessings of God are already ours; in fact, the Apostle Paul teaches us that all the blessings of God are fulfilled in Christ who is our yes and amen (2 Corinthians 1:20 AMP). But in order for the blessings to manifest, we must activate it by our words. We must declare it and proclaim it with great conviction of heart, and this is what I like to call the creating aspect of the believer's life. Again I have to go back and reiterate the point that we are created in God's image and likeness, and even though death entered in by Adam, God restored life back to man through Jesus Christ; therefore, putting us back to the original state he intended for us in the beginning. In the first chapter of Genesis, we see the principle of the power of the spoken word. The earth was described as a mass of darkness and nothingness as in a sense of pure chaos. Out of this state, God was able to create the earth as we now see it. "The earth was without form and an empty waste, and darkness was upon the face of the very great deep. The spirit of God was moving (hovering, brooding) over the face of the waters" (Genesis 1:2, AMP).

The spirit of God was brooding over the face of the waters, and this word *brood* according to Merriam-Webster's Collegiate Dictionary is, "to sit on or hatch eggs, and also to be deep in thought or ponder." And this is what the spirit of God was doing before God the Father spoke anything into being. It is the very same principle we discussed in Bible meditation—the thoughts must be aligned with the Word before we can be effective in our speaking. When this principle is fully understood by the believer, then we will be able to create beauty out of ugliness, strength out of weakness, and order out of chaos. The same spirit that was brooding over the waters is the same spirit dwelling in us; therefore, we will not fail if we will take God at his word. The mind that is renewed with the Word of God gives way to the manifestation of the power of God through the effective, spoken word of God. What we have to realize is that our mouth is not the power, but it is the vessel through which the power flows.

Let us examine a power supply system. The purpose of the power supply system is to provide electricity, which causes many appliances we use on a daily basis to work, such as, our refrigerator, washer and dryer, computer, and, most importantly, lights for us to be able to see in the dark. Even though there may be several outlets that provide electricity, all these outlets lead to one main fuse box. This fuse box is the source where all the power comes from, and through hidden wires and pipes in the walls or ceilings the electricity flows to the individual outlets. If we want to get our room lighted even though there is power from the fuse box to the switch it does not mean that we will get lights in our room by just standing in the room. We will have to turn on the light switch in order for the light to manifest in the room. In the same way the Word of God is like the fuse box that contains all the power necessary to bring light to every dark area our lives. Our mind becomes the power lines through which the Word of God flows, but the vessel to manifest the blessings in our lives is through our mouth. In other words, our mouth is the switch by which the power of God's Word when spoken by us releases the blessings in our lives. The Word of God is so potent and is most powerful when spoken with true revelation of the author of the Word.

DEATH AND LIFE ARE HOUSED IN THE TONGUE

"Death and life are in the power of the tongue, and they who indulge in it shall eat the fruit of it [for death or life]" (Proverbs 18:21, AMP). Let's talk about death for a moment; it is not a topic that many of us like to discuss because it brings with it loss, pain, grief, aloneness, depression, and even ugliness. Yet we as believers do not understand that many of the scenarios we are facing daily are a result of the thoughts we are releasing through our words. For example, "Our kids will never make it in life because of the friends they are hanging out with," or "I will never get that promotion because I am not smart enough," or "My husband will cheat on me because I am getting old," or "I will end up in the hospital because this pain is killing me." God created us to be life giving and creative, but at the fall of man in the Garden of Eden, death entered, and since then creation is going through the process of death. But for the believer, God made a way for us to be able to be life giving and creative again, through Jesus Christ.

We cannot create anything out of chaos if we don't have the source of life, which is the life of Christ flowing in and through us. I urge you, please don't be disillusioned by what you see prospering in the world, my friends, because if it does not have its source in Christ, it will not last, and, of course, the end result will be death. As believers of Jesus Christ, we cannot be running after that which has no foundation in Christ; we need him and him alone in these last days to be able to survive, function, and remain stable. I am often amazed at how we do not have to teach a child to tell lies or cheat or do wrong, but we have to teach them to do the right actions. This is obviously because of the fallen, sinful nature we are born into. Another area is the fact that we don't have to fight to feel bad, depressed, or fearful—these emotions seem to come so easily to us, it's like second nature. All it takes is one negative thought to start a whole downward spiral. The natural response to negative thoughts is for us to speak what we see, and if we are not being filled with the God images, then we are filling up on death images, such as divorce, debt, sickness, and depression. The easiest solution is to call the situation as it is, and, of course, that is what we do most of the time. When all you can see is lack, sickness, poverty, and shortage, how is it possible to speak anything else? That is why the Apostle Paul urges us to fight the good fight of faith. Once we understand that our words are full of power, we will be on the road that starts a progressive journey to the purposeful life.

Now let us discuss life—a new baby laughing, spring time, fresh fruits, green grass, birds chirping, a fresh, crisp crystal river flowing, gentle spring rain, an abundance of flowers. All these descriptions give the image of life, newness, refreshment, peace, and harmony. This is the image God wants us to have of our life, being in a constant state of peace even in the midst of the raging storms, even in the midst of chaos and confusion, even in the midst of lack and shortage, because the fact is that our life is connected to the source of all life and that is Jesus Christ; in fact, Jesus said it this way, "I am the Vine; you are the branches. Whoever lives in Me and I in him bears much (abundant) fruit. However, apart from Me [cut off from vital union with Me] you can do nothing" (John 15:5 AMP).

Our life source will continue to flow once we stay connected to the vine (Jesus Christ). Just like a natural vine that bears grapes, the main vine holds all the extensions of the branches, feeding it sap and letting the branches live—green, young, and productive. It is the branches that produce the fruit because its ability to do this comes from the fact that it is connected to the main vine.

Creativity comes from being connected to the Creator himself; when God came on the scene to create the heavens and the earth in Genesis 1, the place was in chaos and darkness, but God did not say what he saw at that moment in time. God spoke what he wanted to see and this is the creative power of the spoken word. God did not say, "Wow, this place is very dark; I'm not sure I can find my way around here to do anything." No, he took his power-infused words and created something out of nothing, and this very same ability is deposited in us. We have the life-giving words of the Creator available to us to be able to create order out of chaos. So, now, when we are faced with lack, we don't lay back and say how poor we are, or lament that we might as well give up and die now because tomorrow we may lose our house. But instead, we go to the Word and search out the Creator's words like, "My God shall supply all my needs according to his riches in glory" (Philippians 4:19 AMP), and as we practice sourcing the promise we need from God's Word we will be releasing the power necessary to give life to the dead situations around us.

First, we must transform the mental images by getting the life-giving word on the inside of us, and then we will be able to believe God is able; and as we speak those power-infused words of God, beyond a shadow of a doubt, we will be able to see manifestations of that spoken word. The world tells us that we must see to believe, but God's way establishes that believing is seeing. Through the whole creation process God spoke what he wanted to see and then he saw that it was good. Everything that flows out from God will be the best quality. I thank God for the good news being preached around the world today, and as these power-infused words are going out across the nations, God's children are beginning to acquire the revelation that will set chaotic situations in their right order. This, my friends, will usher in the coming of our Lord!

ENJOY LIFE AND SEE GOOD DAYS

"For let him who wants to enjoy life and see good days [good—whether apparent or not] keep his tongue free from evil and his lips from guile (treachery, deceit)" (1 Peter 3:10, AMP).

Many times I hear believers saying that they will only be able to enjoy life when they have accomplished their goals of having a big bank account or acquired their dream house or landed that position in top management. Enjoying life seems to be pushed to the future and is based on the fickle notion that the acquiring of an abundance of material possessions will eventually lead to enjoyment. This concept tends to rob many believers from the quality of life that God intended for them to have now. And though they are in the church, they believe that without these extravagant material possessions life can't be enjoyable. But the Apostle Peter gives us the very simple yet powerful truth by which every believer should base their entire lives on. It does not begin with achieving a status in society or material possessions; it begins with training our tongue to speak those blessings that give life and not death.

Enjoying life now is being able to say, "Even though our situation at home may be a little rough financially, we are so thankful that we have a roof over our heads and food on our table. We may not have everything, but we do have our health and strength and we at least have jobs to go to. Even if we can't take a vacation right now, we are so thankful for quality moments with our children; at least we are not absentee parents. We may not be able to go to the Broadway shows or the five-star restaurants, but we can cook a nice meal and enjoy a family movie with our kids. We may not be able to go to the car wash, but we have opportunities created for us that by washing our cars at home, quality time again is created with our kids that causes a bond that may establish a strong foundation in their lives for the future."

When we learn how to see and speak the way God sees and speaks, then all of the situations that seemed to be difficult before, starts to become easier and enjoyable. But, unfortunately, I have seen parents who could not speak life in the chaos, and they used every free moment to brood over the dead situations. They released words that continued to stifle life until fear and worry overshadowed their present. As a result, they lost special moments that would have created great memories.

The bottom line is that we are all blessed with the power to create, and Proverbs 18:21 states it clearly, that either we will produce life or death by our words. The choice is ours; everything is already done for us through the finished work of Jesus Christ at the cross. His death saved us and his resurrection justifies and equips us for the God-purpose life. Now it is up to us to walk out our lives in this newly given power through the believing and speaking process. If we choose death-words then we will produce death, and if we choose life-words then we will produce life. As we are embarking on this journey to reconstructing our minds and using our life-words, it may be tough in the beginning, but with a long-term commitment to infiltrating our thought life with the power-infused words, this will eventually lead to a consistent, positive speech life as well. As you set forth to accomplish your God-purpose, remember that it all starts with one thought, which can result in life or death, which flows from your mouth. Your mouth is the vessel that transports power; the choice is, ultimately, yours!

POWER THOUGHTS
AND CONFESSIONS

I have the power in me to create by the words I choose to speak.

I choose to speak life words today.

I am connected to the life source, which is the vine (Jesus Christ).

Because I am connected to the vine (Jesus Christ), I will be able to bring creativity and order out of chaos.

I choose to enjoy life today.

I choose to see good days in my life every day because of what I speak.

I will believe God's Word, I will speak God's Word; therefore, I will see God's Word manifest in my natural circumstances today.

My mouth is the vessel for God's power words and the avenue by which I will create life.

WE ARE OVERCOMERS

I have told you these things, so that in Me you may have [perfect] peace and confidence. In the world you have tribulation and trials and distress and frustration; but be of good cheer [take courage; be confident, certain, undaunted]! For I have overcome the world. [I have deprived it of power to harm you and have conquered it for you.]

John 16:33 (AMP)

When we use the word *overcome*, automatically what comes to mind are obstacles. In life there will always be ongoing obstacles, but what really distinguishes the believer is the ability to overcome them. Everyone can overcome, but without the help of Jesus, the overcoming process can and will overburden us at some point, which eventually leads to feelings of shutting down, frustration, and even giving up. Jesus never hides anything from us in his Word. He was very aware of the harsh realities of everyday life. In fact, he was so concerned about us being able to handle it that he spent a great portion of his ministry teaching about everyday issues we will face. He took time to tell us every day will bring its own troubles, trials, and tribulations, but we must learn from him and take heart and be encouraged because we are not alone; and, also, everything we need to overcome, he has provided.

As he tells us about the conflicts we will face, he never leaves us discouraged, alone, or disheartened; he always gave the solution. The overcoming life is obviously one that is lived in Christ; every day we have to remind ourselves by saying it out loud so we can hear ourselves say, "Today, my life is lived in Christ."

Without that reassurance, we will have to resort to our abilities to overcome, and, my friends, this life truly requires more than our smarts, abilities, and strategies. We need the favor of God to overcome. The days are becoming more brutal, the downturn in the economy—which is affecting the job markets, foreclosure of homes, and the rising cost of bare necessities are clear indications that we cannot survive on mere human abilities. We must realize the times we are living in and understand that God is positioning the church for his return. Will things get better? With God all things are possible; but if we are going to wait for things to get better to enjoy life and then trust God, we are heading in the wrong direction. If better conditions are going to determine the quality of life we live now, then there truly will be no need for the word *overcome* to exist in our vocabulary. The overcomer in Christ gets the opportunity to show forth the God they serve to a world that is in great need of him. I am not saying to glory in loss, poverty, or lack. What I am saying is that we obviously have distressing situations to deal with, but in the midst of it we have a chance to put our faith in the one who already overcame and has promised us that we will overcome because of him.

HOW DO WE OVERCOME?

Jesus overcame the world for us, but we still have to deal with the obstacles presented before us, so the question still remains, "How do we overcome?" I am always amazed that no matter what topic we bring up in our everyday life, the Bible has the answer for it. And what really gets my attention is the consistency of God's instruction to the believer in dealing with it. I have stated that the new covenant believer's work is to believe and speak, and that does not change no matter what the situation is. I have a great passion for the Word of God because it is sustenance to the believer. In my office as a pastor I see the discouragement and frustration in many believers because they have not been able to overcome their situations, and the root cause of the frustration is their focus on the fickle words, opinions, and promises of men. One of my greatest desires is to see the believer live out this overcoming life that God intended for them to have. The reason I am passionate about this is because I was a victim of this said scenario. I was always looking to and hanging on to the empty promises made to me by people who I thought held a good position, or who even appeared to possess much wisdom, yet I always found myself coming up empty and sorely disappointed. And if I seem to reiterate some points, it is because I care deeply for the body of Christ and I know that the constant teaching of the truth can and will definitely set God's people free.

Now, this mindset that man's opinions are more important than God's words in our lives causes us to build on a very shaky foundation, and pretty much we end up on a see-saw ride throughout our lives. The truth about this design is that it will cause us to fail, or, more so, not walk out the God-purpose for our lives, and the reason I say this is because man lives life out of an abundance of feelings, and most of the time our words are generated from how we are feeling at the moment. For example, today, if I feel happy, I could boost your confidence, and tomorrow if I feel down I can cause you to be crushed because I am always changing. This is why Jesus urges us to build our foundation on the rock, and this rock is Jesus himself because he is never changing and knows what we need to fulfill this purpose he has called us to.

THERE ARE TWO WEAPONS IN OUR POSSESSION TO OVERCOME

And they have overcome (conquered) him by means of the blood of the Lamb and by the utterance of their testimony, for they did not love and cling to life even when faced with death (holding their lives cheap till they had to die for their witnessing).

Revelation 12:11 (AMP)

1)THE BLOOD OF THE LAMB ESTABLISHES WHO WE BELONG TO

This is the first and most important weapon made available to us as believers. In fact, it is the most powerful weapon in the overcoming life. Why do I make such a bold statement? Because the blood of the lamb establishes who we belong to. The blood of the lamb marks us as his chosen and sets us apart as God's children. It not only sets us apart, but it provides protection as well. Oh how precious is the blood of the lamb; when we truly get a revelation of the preciousness of the price we were bought with, the only result would be the overcoming life. Many times the enemy gains easy access into the believer's life because of the lack of understanding of the blood of the lamb. The Lamb of God was perfect in every way, and to be perfect it means sin must be nonexistent. This is the power of the blood, because it took perfection to purchase imperfection.

Jesus Christ's shed blood was the price that was paid for our freedom. And this is the reason we are able to stand in God's presence unafraid and also enjoy all his blessings. It is what we call the redemption plan. Once sin entered into creation, we became slaves to the fallen nature, and in order for a slave to go free, a price had to be paid. The price of our freedom from sin required the blood of the lamb. It is the blood of the lamb that justifies us or acquits us from a guilty verdict and allows right standing with God. We do not have to come to God fearful of punishment anymore because the Lamb of God satisfied the wrath of God in full. In fact, the blood of the lamb was an over payment for our sins, therefore, we can be confident when we come before God that he will hear us. He doesn't hear us because we are good in ourselves or because of our good works, he hears us because of the blood of the lamb that is applied to us as a result of our acceptance of the Lamb of God. The Apostle Paul declares that we were not redeemed with corruptible things like silver or gold, but we were redeemed by the precious blood of the lamb. To *redeem* simply means to "buy back," so we can now say we were bought back with a price, which is the blood of the Lamb of God. Having established that a price was paid for us, we should now start to understand that we have a new owner—or we now belong to someone. The good news is that we now belong to the King of kings and Lord of lords, and he did not purchase our freedom to bring us back to slavery, but he paid for us to be forever free. It is the best arrangement anyone could ask for, and it is truly what we call a divine exchange; only the precious blood of our Lord and Savior Jesus Christ could accomplish such a task.

We cannot truly live everyday life victoriously without grasping the truth about the blood of the lamb. It is the blood of the lamb that states very clearly who we belong to, and when that statement is understood in the mind and heart of the believer, holding our position of right standing with God becomes the very foundation of our existence. The enemy constantly attacks our right standing with God by bringing us away from the truth about our identity. The enemy's plan is to constantly bring us back to the sin nature, the slavery mentality that we always have to try to be good or else God will not work out present difficult situations for us; he likes to use our past failures and faults to bring us away from our rightful position of right standing with God.

In order to overcome in this life, we have to keep ever before us faith in the blood of the lamb and its ability to keep us right with God. The moment we move away from the blood of the Lamb of God we enter into the zone of self-effort, and this road will only lead us to defeat. Self-effort is based on our ability to please God without the way of his Son, and no amount of work on our part can ever impress God or please him. Unfortunately, the enemy is always looking for an entrance to pull us away, and this is his cheap shot that he takes every single time. He is called the accuser and he loves to get the believer to a place of introspection; it is here that we become weakened and unable to fight the good fight of faith. But believers equipped with the revelation of the blood of the lamb are forces to reckon with because the foundation on which they stand is built on God's system and not that of the world. They are able to remain and stand firm in the fact that they belong to the one who paid a price that they could never repay, yet they are never made to feel guilty about it; however, they hold fast to their true identity of being in Christ.

2) THE WORD OF OUR TESTIMONY ESTABLISHES WHOSE AUTHORITY WE STAND ON

The second weapon granted to the believer is the spoken word. It is not very difficult to speak with authority when we know who we are. While the blood of the lamb establishes who we belong to, the word of our testimony establishes whose authority we stand on. For example, if my father is the king of a county and I go out through the palace, I do not have to explain to everyone whom I am. The fact that I bear my father's name speaks volume to the onlookers, and they know very well whom I belong to. If I take the podium and give a command, I will not be questioned because everyone knows that I speak on the authority of my father, and the fact that I bear his mark and I speak in his name, I have all authority just as if the king himself was speaking. But, the issue at hand is that most of the time the believer knows the power of the blood and the price with which they were bought; they know all the benefits that come with salvation, yet they are not able to overcome in possessing by right what is theirs, thereby resulting in defeat.

A majority of our time is spent on trying to figure out why there are so many negative results, even though we are born again and not enough time on taking the authority we possess and using it against the wiles of the enemy. For example, we give ear to the voice of condemnation that tells us because of past sins we committed, such us lying, cheating, or gossiping that caused afflictions on others has caused the obstacles in our lives. You see, the enemy doesn't mind if we call ourselves Christians; he does not mind even if we go to church often to praise and pray on Sunday, because these religious acts do not seem to pose much of a threat to him as long as we do not possess our rightful authority. But, a believer that understands whom they belong to and whose authority they stand on beats the enemy to the ground every time, because when we infuse our words with the power and authority of the king, they become words that will decimate every ill plan, purpose, and intention of the stealer of our God-purpose. This is such a powerful truth and God makes it simple for us; he did not say that once you are born again, you must take a trip to boot camp and do two years of self-defense courses. No, he teaches us through his Word to build faith and confidence in his promises, then when the difficult situations present themselves, we will be able to speak those promises that we are equipped with to overcome them.

Over a period of time, the library of our past gets filled with volumes of testimonies in picture form, and every new level of warfare or every new obstacle is now viewed by the believer as a new opportunity for taking more ground in the overcoming life. As we continue to build on this principle, we will be able to release authority and power through our mouths, that which we already believe in our hearts; we will also be able to experience deliverance from our past hurts and pains, thereby becoming a living testimony that today we are still standing.

Our testimony of the goodness of God in spite of hopeless situations and circumstances are like poison to the enemy, because he always banks on us taking the natural response when we face troubles by confessing what we see. It puts him in a state of chaos when a believer can maintain confidence in God and keep expressing that confidence verbally. The only way the enemy is allowed to gain strength over us is when we stay quiet and don't engage our mouths with the promises of God and the testimony of our past deliverances. He loves to see us frustrate the grace of God by declaring how unworthy we are; he also enjoys a believer that lives a life of regret, and it is very likely that we will speak words to match up with these images. But I thank God for the power of the spoken word, which went into effect with Christ being raised from the dead. Jesus fulfilled all the work by keeping the law perfectly, and from that point on, God the Father made us joint heirs with Christ, sharing in his inheritance. The whole walk in the new covenant cannot be lived without the ability to speak the Word. The power of the spoken word is revolutionizing to the life of the believer, and once this revelation is established, it would be able to effect change from the inside out.

POWER THOUGHTS AND CONFESSIONS

Even though I may have trials and tribulations in everyday life, I am assured that Jesus Christ overcame the world for me.

Today I am equipped with the tools to overcome the trials that may arise.

I know who I belong to and my position of right standing today is not based on me and my abilities, but it is wrapped up in the precious blood of Jesus Christ.

Today I will speak God's Word with authority over every situation that may present itself to keep me from moving forward.

I am determined to overcome every wile of the devil with the blood of the lamb and with the word of my testimony.

Today I refuse to speak what I see in the natural, but I choose to speak the promises of God for my life.

I may be down today, but I declare that I will not stay down in Jesus's name.

I know and understand that in everything that is happening in my life I am more than a conqueror through Jesus Christ my Lord.

REMEMBERING AND FORGETTING GOD'S WAY

To remember something simply means to revisit a past event and ponder on it, much like meditation, as discussed in the earlier chapters. The memory is a very beautiful and intricate part of the human being. The memory is not our enemy; it was actually created by God for a specific purpose. Our memory was created to house the kindness, goodness, and grandeur of our great God, but after the fall of man the memory became somewhat corrupted and, as a result, we don't have to try very hard to remember the bad things that have happened to us. As a matter of fact, hashing up the negatives almost seems like second nature to us. The memory has a great role to play in fulfilling the God-purpose for which we were created. One of the greatest weapons also formed against the believer is a warped remembering pattern, because the enemy knows that if we could be kept in this state of revisiting the past, we would never be able to move forward into the glorious future God has planned out for us.

The memory is a canvas where life pictures are displayed; it is supposed to be a canvas of rich colors that radiate life, fullness, peace, wholeness, joy, hope, and creativity.

Unfortunately, the canvas has been smeared by the enemy with pictures of darkness, ugliness, and constant loads of heaviness. Granted, we have all had bad experiences, sometimes even detestable experiences, and the enemy has majored in getting us to engrave the images of these experiences in our memory. Sometimes the effect of the bad experiences that have happened to us seems to be ever lurking on the sidelines, even though we are consciously making an effort to erase them from our memory. They may be so deeply rooted that even a certain scent, color, or season can trigger the whole scenario anew. Many times the past seems to be the major hindrance for moving forward for many of us. I know the question that may be popping into your minds at this present time as you are reading this is, "How am I supposed to forget these images engraved in my memory, when what happened to me was real and it caused me real pain?"

The truth is, God does not expect you to forget your past; in fact, he asked us to remember our past but not in the way we do presently. I started saying that the memory was created to house the images of the greatness of our God. Let us look at how the Lord instructs us to use our memory.

And [earnestly] remember that you were a servant in the land of Egypt and that the Lord your God brought you out from there with a mighty hand and an outstretched arm; therefore the

> Lord your God commanded you to observe and
> take heed to the Sabbath day.
>
> Deuteronomy 5:15 (AMP)

God instituted specific days for certain feasts to be celebrated by the Jewish people, in order for them to never forget the goodness of him in their lives. After the children of Israel left Egypt, God instructed them to observe the Sabbath. This was not just for ritual sake; this would bring to their memory the fact that the God of the universe saved their lives from major destruction by bringing them out of slavery, where they had to work continuously, into freedom—that now they did not have to be subjected to the harsh hand of the slave master. Among this observance there are seven feasts celebrated by the Jewish people yearly, and every one of those feasts surrounds a major event concerning the greatness of God. For us Christians, Jesus instituted the Lord's Supper as a way of remembering the act that would totally set us free from the bondage of sin and death and cause a free flow of healing, even to our physical bodies. We remember Calvary's cross for the purpose of grasping the depth of revelation embedded in the divine exchange that took place two thousand years ago.

God's way of remembering brings with it a substantial amount of blessings and inner peace, which gives us the picture of rest and refreshment. The only way to find rest is to know that the troubles from the past and the troubles at hand are being taken care of by someone we trust, and this rest allows us to shift our focus to the true source of our happiness, which is Jesus, thereby taking the stress and pressure off ourselves.

When we choose to remain focused on the negative memories, it will direct us on a path of self-victimization and introspection. But, the good news is that if we made it out of that terrible situation, it means that there are some positives we can take away with us. God can take any broken situation and turn it around in our favor. God does not ask us to forget everything we've been through in our past and act like it never existed. The truth is that it does exist, but the way we choose to view it will determine the expected end. Where we are today is a result of the situations and circumstances of the past. Where we are going tomorrow will be determined by what we choose to take from the past.

FORGETTING GOD'S WAY

It will stand then to reason that if there is a way to remember then there most certainly must be a way to forget. In my own life I can say that many times I tried to forget my past—both afflictions that were done to me and afflictions that I caused on others. And even though I said I forgot about it, the mere mention of a name from the past could send me into a downward spiral. Our way of forgetting is, oftentimes, not

healthy, and it seems as if we go around in a circle by return-
ing to the same point we started off from. Sometimes we try
to forget by pretending on the surface everything is fine
while on the inside there is a whirlwind of emotions, or we
try to ignore the experience by not speaking about the experience or the people who were involved in hurting us. As I
shared earlier, my life had been one that was plagued with
hurts, abuses, and insecurities due to the absence of a real
father. Although I was in the church I did not have a renewed mind with the word of God, and the security I was
looking for did not originate from the promises of God. I
thought, maybe if I got married to a young man who was in
the church like myself I would definitely be secure. At age
twenty-three I got married only to realize that there are no
perfect people, and six years later I was divorced because the
perfection and peace I was searching for could only come
from a perfect God. The truth is; no one is perfect and I never really forgot about my past; I had only ignored my past by
trying to replace it with other relationships. That broken
marriage left yet another bruise in my memory, and I took
on another dose of condemnation. It drove me to further
despair and rebellion toward God. I like to explain it like
this: instead of eradicating the problem, we put it into a closet and close the door, so from the outside, to everyone else,
everything seems normal, neat, and organized, and the only
person who knows what is going on behind that closet door
is us. And the point is that we keep adding to this closet and

closing the door, keeping it all safe in there—at least so we chose to believe—and then one day someone comes along and mentions a name and that name is the key that unlocks that closet door, and everything that is stored comes crashing down.

The man that God used so powerfully to release me from the bondage I lived in was the Apostle Paul. I have the greatest love for him because he exuded a unique passion, and, to me, this was the defining quality that sets him apart. His passion extended to the extremes—both against and for the gospel of Jesus Christ. Let us imagine together his life. Though there are many great books written about the Apostle Paul, I would only attempt to give a synopsis of this great man's life and how it has impacted not only me but the generations before. According to the book of Acts of the apostles, Paul was a man with a great wealth of knowledge; he was a Pharisee, so the extent of his knowledge of the law was vast. Paul was present at the stoning of Stephen, and he was determined to stop anyone that would try to bring any other doctrine than that which was already established. His reputation was synonymous with the persecution of the early church disciples. He was so relentless in accomplishing this task that he traveled to Damascus in pursuit of Christ followers; he was feared by many. But on his journey to Damascus he had an encounter with his maker; you see, his past was not about to stop his God-purpose.

Paul had a divine encounter with God, and I must note here that one cannot have a divine meeting with God and not be changed. There is a divine appointment with God for each and every one of us; it is a time appointed by God to bring us face to face with him, to confront and activate the God-purpose in our lives. The way it happens for us today is not, or may not be, the way it happened to the Apostle Paul, but it can come in the form of us taking up an invitation to attend a church service or even a coworker sharing the good news with us. Whatever form this appointment comes in, I can assure you that it will take place, because this encounter is what empowers us to walk into our God-purpose.

After his encounter with God, Paul was given clear instructions as to the journey he must now follow, but we must pay attention to the fact that his past is not eradicated and God does not cause memory loss to everyone around. His past, in reality, causes a switch from him being the persecutor to becoming the persecuted. God did not remove anything from his past, nor did he change his personality, his drive, or his passion. God used those very strengths to accomplish his will for his life, and when the Lord touches us in this way, how we access our memory becomes the very foundation of success. Though he faced many trials and tribulations of beatings, being shipwrecked, imprisoned, and, finally, beheaded, it did not stop the God-purpose for his life. If Paul did not choose to forget God's way he would have become a victim of his past, and his life and God-purpose would have been aborted. Paul's decision to forget God's way, equipped him to write three-fourths of the New Testament, and most of it for us Gentiles. Now this is what I call fulfilling the God-purpose. What was his key to achieving this God-purpose? Granted, there are many major qualities that we can pull form Paul's life that would attribute to his success in walking out his God-purpose, but for me it is all wrapped up in the book of Philippians where Paul chooses to forget God's way:

> [For my determined purpose is] that I may know Him [that I may progressively become more deeply and intimately acquainted with Him, perceiving and recognizing and understanding the wonders of His Person more strongly and more clearly], and that I may in that same way come to know the power outflowing from His resurrection [which it exerts over believers], and that I may so share His sufferings as to be continually transformed [in spirit into His likeness even] to His death, [in the hope] That if possible I may attain to the [spiritual and moral] resurrection [that lifts me] out from among the dead [even while in the body]. Not that I have now attained [this ideal], or have already been made perfect, but I press on to lay hold of (grasp) and make my own, that for which Christ Jesus (the Messiah) has laid hold of me and made me His own. I do not consider, brethren, that I have captured and made it my own [yet]; *but one thing I do [it is my one aspira-*

tion]: forgetting what lies behind and straining forward to what lies ahead, I press on toward the goal to win the [supreme and heavenly] prize to which God in Christ Jesus is calling us upward.

Philippians 3:10-14
(AMP, words in italics from author)

My friends, we cannot have rest and peace on the inside if we are constantly carrying around the heavy burden of hurts, pains, and disappointments. Let us make a choice and embrace God's way of remembering and forgetting. Let us look at the past and see how the hand of God brought us out of it. Let us ponder and give deep thought to the goodness of God, that we survived, and it is still God who is carrying us today. When we make this choice, we will be empowered to overcome the negative thought cycle and rebuild new memories, even from the worst of conditions. I have learnt this life lesson from the Apostle Paul and I chose to look back on my past life of being divorced, abused and broken and take from it all the graciousness of God. Today I write from a place of healing and wholeness while fulfilling my God-purpose, which is to help set others free also. One thing I know for sure and I encourage you today; believe that God is faithful to his promises, and if you stay in faith he will bring his promises to pass in your life. Use your memory to exalt and lift high the God who brought you through.

POWER THOUGHTS
AND CONFESSIONS

I am very thankful today for my memory.

I declare that my memory is a canvas of bright and radiant colors.

I refuse to let the enemy paint on the canvas of my memory.

I reject every negative memory that triggers fear, hurt, and rejection in my life.

I choose to revisit the past and celebrate the greatness of God in every bad situation I have faced.

I am determined to take from my past memories only the positives that will give me strength to go on.

I will not carry into the future the memories of the people who hurt me.

Today I choose to remember God's way.

Today I choose to forget God's way.

KNOW THE LORD
IS WITH YOU

"And I will ask the Father and He will give you another Comforter (Counselor, Helper, Intercessor, Advocate, Strengthener, and Standby), that He may remain with you forever" (John 14:16, AMP).

One of the most important keys to fulfilling your God-purpose is knowing that the Lord is with you. It is an awesome feeling to know you have support in the natural sphere of life like family, friends, coworkers, peers, and acquaintances, and be that as it may, the ingredient in making this phase perfect is knowing that the Creator of the universe, the one who brings the world as we know it into existence out of non-existence goes before you and backs you up. With this kind of knowledge, there is no way to fail, but there is an assurance that the very purpose you were created for will come to be a reality, because the one who authored it is with you.

I would like to break it down to our reality so we can get a clearer picture of the spiritual truth that is existent in this kind of knowledge. For example, a child will face many new phases in his or her lifetime, and one of the most common phases to all children is the very first day of school; it seems to trigger their realization of their first step into independence. It can be a very fearful period due to the unknown of the environment; unknown, new faces and personalities; the fear of separation from the familiar and what they know as a safe haven of home; the fear of a lack of ability to undertake the new task ahead; fear of disappointing their parents; fear of a lack of protection and comfort; etc. But in the midst of all this uncertainty, anxiety, and fears, what makes it easier for the child is when the parents reassure the child that all will be well because they will accompany them on this new venture. This knowledge on the child's part allows an immediate release from the unseen internal pressure and can cause the child to look forward to undertaking the challenge. This kind of knowledge that they are not alone can boost confidence and birth joy, thereby removing fears of the unknown. The point here is that if we as earthly parents understand this principle and place emphasis on reassuring our earthly children, then how much more will our heavenly Father do toward us. This nurturing and caring aspect in us originates from the Father of all fathers. We are still subject to make mistakes. What a powerful revelation it would be for us to have and maintain that the Lord is with us. Imagine the endless possibilities that would be made available to us in just us having this kind of knowledge.

As I have explored the Bible about the lives of the many men and women God chose to use, I found that the common denominator was that the Lord was with them. God used ordinary, and even the least of men, and women to accomplish great feats that would preserve future generations. I love to read the Bible and see that some of the men and women were just like you and me. They had faults and flaws; however, these short comings did not keep them from accomplishing their God-purpose. We must remember; in order to fulfill the God-purpose, we must have God in it. If we don't have God in it, then it would just be purpose, but the believer lives his or her life to fulfill the God-purpose.

My God-purpose is to bring the message of the gospel to God's children; and I am a pastor that truly believes in keeping things real. The fact that I bring good news establishes that there are existing, bad situations. So I don't bring good news to say that you will never have troubles, trials, or tribulations, but, in fact, I bring good news in the midst of your bad situations to show you that you don't have to stay that way. There is hope, faith, and love in the middle of all this chaos, and you can experience ongoing peace. I find that many times the cause of our heartaches, disappointments, and frustrations is due to the message that says you will never have a bad moment in life again. This message leaves believers very discouraged and confused as to why God did not change things for them, and why he didn't make it all go away. My Lord, in his teachings, explained that in this world you will have trials and troubles but take heart or be encouraged because he has already overcome them for you (John 16:33, AMP).

Jesus does not want us disillusioned; he wants us to have confidence in him that he will be with us through it all. How else would we know he is with us if we never face any trails or hard times? How would we see the greatness of God manifested in our lives if there are no opportunities for him to show up and show forth himself strong on our behalf? How would others get to see the demonstration of God's power if he has no avenue to work through? My friends, we are the avenue that God has chosen to shine forth his glory to a people that is in desperate need of him. It would do us good to shift our knowledge from our abilities to the knowledge of our Creator's abilities. Let us take some time out and explore the lives of a few people in the Bible who fulfilled their God-purpose.

JOSEPH MADE A WAY OF SURVIVAL FOR HIS PEOPLE (GENESIS, CHAPTERS 37-50, AMP)

From a very early age, Joseph's God-purpose was made very clear to him in two consecutive dreams from the Lord. Joseph was dearly loved by his earthly father, and this realization generated hatred from his brothers. This hatred, in turn, caused them to sell Joseph into slavery, thereby removing him from the inheritance they thought he would be liable to receive, and it severed the very source that fueled Joseph's confidence, which was his father's love for him. Let's imagine together here that Joseph stands in the middle of a slave market, stripped of his colorful coat and wearing nothing but his underwear. He stands in the public domain being scrutinized by the potential buyers for signs of diseases that might pose a threat to their well-being should they decided to purchase him.

Joseph is then purchased and taken to serve Potiphar—the captain of Pharaoh's guard—and while serving there, it was evident to all around, including Potiphar, that the Lord was with Joseph. Potiphar was able to identify and state this fact because he could see that everything Joseph did prospered, but, even though Joseph was prospering, the forces against the God-purpose were at work on an overtime schedule, trying desperately to abort the plans of the Maker for Joseph's life. He was falsely accused of rape and sentenced to prison, but, yet again, he did not let his circumstances keep him from accomplishing the God-purpose. I believe Joseph held onto the fact that the Lord was with him and that the Lord would never let him down. He even prospered and was promoted in the prison.

While Joseph held onto the truth that the Lord was with him, he was able to maintain good work ethics, build faith, and learn how to use the gifting in him. He learned how to be faithful with little, how to be a good steward over whatever jurisdiction was awarded to him, and this quality allowed him the capability of remaining humble yet confident that the dream he had in his life would be a definite. Joseph's confidence stemmed from the knowledge that the Lord was with him, and when the time was right, the dream would become a reality. Joseph did get the opportunity to stand before Pharaoh and display the God-gift of interpreting dreams and, as a result of this God-ability, God-purpose was unfolding. Because the Lord was with Joseph, he was able to exercise wisdom that would save many lives—not only that of his own people, but the foreigners who he served as well. Joseph was promoted as chief minister to Pharaoh, and with this position he was able to secure food and land for the said brothers that sold him in the first place. Most of the time, fulfilling the God-purpose in our lives does not mean that we would be free from trials and troubles; in fact, it is these very said trials and troubles that help to mold us into the vessel that God can work through. My friends, the present situations that we face in our lives should not deter us from fulfilling the God-purpose, *because we as believers are equipped with assurance of knowing that God is with us.*

Joshua Leads the Israelites into the Promised Land
(The Book of Joshua, AMP)

Joshua was part of the original group of Israelites that left Egypt and followed Moses to the wilderness. He was often made reference to as Moses's assistant. He saw firsthand the greatness of God as Moses demonstrated the many signs and wonders in reasoning with Pharaoh to let God's people go. Joshua stood at the border of the Red Sea and had the opportunity to see Pharaoh's army coming after them with nowhere to go for safety; and in that brief moment of hopelessness, the God of Israel opened up a dry path that allowed their lives to be saved. Joshua was one of the eye-witnesses of the Promised Land because he was used as a spy to scout the land and bring back evidence that the promise of God is based on truth. At that moment, even with evidence that the Word of God was true, he was turned against by the majority that demanded his life.

Imagine the devastation Joshua and Caleb might have felt at that moment, having hardcore evidence that the promise exists but not being able to possess it because of man's opinion. We must stop and admire Joshua and his friend Caleb because in the midst of such great tragedy they never lost sight of their God-purpose. They held onto the hope of possessing what God had prepared for them. Perhaps if we had faced the same situation like Joshua and Caleb we would have said, "There is no need to press on to fulfill this God purpose for our lives. It just looks like a waste of time to continue chasing this dream that now seems impossible to attain," yet when we look at the big picture, Joshua never gave up; he held fast to the fact that the Lord was with them and it was going to happen. Even though unbelief existed among the majority of the people and caused a major delay in possessing the land, it did not deter Joshua from *knowing* it was going to come to pass. Perhaps he did not have a clue that he would be chosen to lead the people to possess the land, but he had to know for sure that he was going to get to that land because God promised it.

After Moses's death, Joshua was commanded by the Lord to prepare himself and the people to go in and take the land. I am sure God knew Joshua had fears and concerns about being capable of handling the purpose at hand, because three times the Lord told Joshua to be courageous and strong.

We need to always keep in mind that God calls men and women like you and me; the people of the Bible were people just like us—they experienced fears, anxiety, worry, frustration, depression, anger, and probably even mood swings. But, the defining factor in all of their lives was the fact that they knew the Lord was with them. Joshua was able to lead his people into the Promised Land and take possession of the city. They definitely did not possess or take this new territory the conventional way by going in initially to fight. But they went in with the presence of the Lord and marched around the city wall for seven days—six of those days they said nothing—and on the seventh day Joshua told them to shout, and they shouted and those walls that were keeping them out of the reality of the God-purpose came crashing down, giving them the greatest victory they could ever imagine.

My friends, being able to fulfill the God-purpose in our lives may never happen the way we think it should happen, but when we know that the Lord is with us, it does not matter how it is going to happen, but, rather, it matters that we know who is with us while it is happening.

DAVID BECAME KING
(1 AND 2 SAMUEL; 1 KINGS AND 1 CHRONICLES, AMP)

I am not quite sure David saw the signs of kingship for himself even though it was set in his destiny, but one thing we know for sure is that in his youth he loved the Lord. Though he was hidden in the fields with his shepherding gears, it did not stop him from knowing his God had a great purpose for his life. I like to think of him as a unique and humble character, not caring so much about being on the world stage in order to serve well, but serving for an audience of one.

The fields were his stage and he performed daily without hesitation and with precise perfection, because he knew the one who would ultimately have the final approval was the only one he was concerned with pleasing. Though he did not have the accolades to his name and was pushed aside because of his youth, he did not use that reasoning to become rebellious toward his maker. David was a man definitely marked for greatness but hidden in the outdoors far away from the social limelight, yet was able to write some of the most beautiful, heartfelt, love songs that we still sing today to our heavenly Father, taken from the book of Psalms. No one was there to see him protect his flock by attacking the lion and bear; it did not make the headline news, but this did not stop him from serving. He was used for delivering food to his brothers who were presumably stronger and more important than he was. But the world's ways and systems are not the Lord's ways. The Lord had a purpose for David's life and it was up to God to equip him to live out that purpose. God chose to use the simple act of serving food to his brothers to put David in the right place at the right time.

Sometimes it is in the simple acts of serving others that we find our God-purpose. Here he is serving food for his not-so-happy brothers; while there with the food he recognizes that the one who is most important to him is being made a mockery of and no one is brave enough to take a stand. God's purpose will always cause us to defend our Maker, and when we choose to do that we will always have the backing of our Maker. Because David knew that the Lord was with him, he could whip out his slingshot with five smooth stones and he knew it would work to bring this giant down. Our confidence cannot originate and be established in our abilities, that is why the God-purpose is different from just purpose. The God-purpose needs God to make it work, not our abilities; God will enhance what we have when we have confidence in his abilities to get it done. It took some years before David took his throne over the united kingdom of Israel and it was not without many trials and tribulations, but David had the knowledge that the Lord was with him.

THE LORD IS WITH YOU

The Bible is filled with numerous characters and they all had a God-purpose to fulfill. Those who knew the Lord was with them did fulfill their purpose, and those who did not believe and instead trusted in their own abilities failed to fulfill their God-purpose. There are many lives you can read about: Moses, Gideon, Elijah, Elisha, Jabez, King Jehosphat, Niomi, Ruth, Boaz, Hannah, Samuel, John the Baptist, the apostles—Peter, James, John, and Paul, just to name a few.

I want to encourage you, more than anything else, to know that the Lord is with you. It is most difficult to comprehend a child being born into this world and a mother and father walking away and leaving the child alone to face things on their own, and even though there may be cases of this scenario, most parents try their best to stay and nurture their children. So let me place before you, food for thought. If our earthly parents understand this principle and try their best to fulfill it in the child's life, how much more will your heavenly Father, who wrote the plan out for your life, bring this God-purpose to a reality. We stand to reason then that once we understand we were created on purpose for purpose there is absolutely no way God will leave us alone, but in fact he will be with us every step of the way.

I challenge you today to walk away from the old way of thinking, find for yourself a good Bible teaching, Christ-centric church that teaches the power of the cross, the blood, and the finished work and person of Jesus Christ, and start anew. It is never too late in God's eyes; as a matter of fact, he waits with open arms for you to come home. He has not forgotten about you or the purpose for which he created you in the first place. God is not looking for every opportunity to discipline you; he is looking for every opportunity to bring you home to him and his purpose for you. Maybe you have strayed away from your God-purpose because of disappointments in your life. Perhaps the pressures of not being able to keep all the laws have caused rebellion in your heart toward the church and God. My friends, God loves you immensely and to prove his love he gave us the most precious gift, which is his Son Jesus Christ, and in Jesus Christ we have all that we need to face this life and to fulfill our God-purpose. All you have to do is accept the way your heavenly father has made for you and come into the fullness, wholeness, and peace of God, and know that the Lord is with you!

> Let your character or moral disposition be free from love of money [including greed, avarice, lust, and craving for earthly possessions] and be satisfied with your present [circumstances and with what you have]; for He [God] Himself has said, I will not in any way fail you nor give you up nor leave you without support. [I will] not, [I will] not, [I will] not in any degree leave you helpless nor forsake nor let [you] down (relax My hold on you)! [Assuredly not!]
>
> Hebrews 13:5 (AMP)

POWER THOUGHTS AND CONFESSIONS

I am assured and I know with great confidence that the Lord is with me.

I am determined to fulfill my God-purpose—not in my strength and abilities, but in the Lord's strength and abilities.

Even though my natural circumstances are not lining up with the God-purpose right now, I will not be discouraged, but I hold onto the truth that the Lord is with me.

I thank God for the men of old like Joseph, Joshua, and King David, that I will fulfill my God-purpose, and if they overcame the worst of conditions so can I, because the Lord is with me.

I have God's promise today that he will never leave me nor forsake me, and because of this promise I will fulfill my God-purpose.

I proclaim and declare with great latitude that I am created on propose for a God-purpose!

Bibliography

Leaf, Dr. Caroline. *Who Switched Off my Brain?* Southlake, TX: Inprov, Ltd, 2009.

Mitchell, Dr. Marva. *It Takes a Church to Raise a Village.* Shippensburg, PA: Destiny Image Publishing, Inc., 2001.

Merriam-Webster's Collegiate Dictionary, Eleventh Edition. Springfield, MA: Merriam-Webster Inc., 2003.

Vine's Concise Dictionary of the Bible. Nashville, TN: Thomas Nelson, Inc., 1997, 1999.

ABOUT THE AUTHOR

Lisa Singh is the pastor of
Heavenly Grace Ministries in New York.
She had been a contributing writer for the
Carribbean Star Newspaper. She is the host of Living the
POP Life—*People of Prayer believing in the Power of
Prayer*...aired weekdays on www.globespanradio.com
Lisa lives in Queens with her husband and two children.

www. hgmny.org

37400637R00093

Made in the USA
Middletown, DE
01 December 2016